"*Super Health* is ideal for people of all ages and levels of health. The principles and practical advice imparted by K.C. are consistent with today's leading-edge scientific research and are a guide and inspiration for anyone seeking to improve their health and performance."

LEONARD SMITH, M.D., FACS, Retired Practitioner
of General and Vascular Surgery and Nutritional Medicine

"*Super Health* is the single most comprehensive health book I've ever read by a *huge* margin. K.C. has ingeniously transformed the concept behind his perfect food, The Living Fuel, into the ideal health book. Indeed, the many pearls of wisdom in this book are *living* words that actually *speak to you!* K.C. is literally years ahead of his time, and we are the fortunate beneficiaries of his hard work. Read this book and prosper!"

DR. MICHAEL A. COREY, author of *The God Hypothesis*

"My life has been changed dramatically through K.C.'s insight and wisdom in nutrition. This book should be made required reading for medical and nursing school curriculums, because it will reduce sickness and disease and increase life spans. K.C. is part of God's master plan to touch people so they can extend their quality of life through nutrition."

PHILLIP GOLDFEDDER, M.D., Neurosurgeon,
Author of *Healing Is Yours*

"Since following the Seven Golden Keys of K.C.'s *Super Health* and taking his Living Fuel at the age of 54, I have slept better and optimized my weight. It has been a catalyst for me to return to fighting and to defend my world championship title. K.C. has changed my life."

JAMES SISCO, Eight-Time World Kickboxing Champion

"I am living proof that good nutrition, exercise, and the other principles laid out by K.C. Craichy will turn your life around. You don't have to feel sick and tired all the time. As you apply this knowledge, you will learn that K.C. can help you go to the next le

ROD MOORE, Retired U.S. Army

D1041916

"K.C. is one of the most respectable authorities on organic nutrition in the world today. The nutritional products he has helped to create I recommend to the very best professional and Olympic athletes in the world as well as to anyone desiring upgrades in their choices of food."

BOB COOLEY, Author of *The Genius of Flexibility 1.0*, Founder of The Meridian Flexibility System™

"At the age of twenty-five, I was diagnosed with Crohn's disease. Eating high fiber, healthy food was very difficult for me to digest, so my diet was very limited. The Seven Golden Keys program helped me not only digest all types of food, but it has also given me back the energy that was robbed through a depleted immune system. I thank the Lord for K.C. and this program!"

CHERI HENLEY, Musician and Mother

"K.C. is a champion for the health of the whole family. As a former healthcare professional and now homeschooling mother, I am constantly faced with how to balance the demands of a busy family with the needs for a healthy lifestyle. He not only tells you how to achieve a healthier lifestyle, but he formulated the products to complete the job. We are continually inspired by his passion for God-honoring nutrition and wellness for all people. Unlike other diet programs, the Seven Golden Keys touch my life both physically and spiritually. Thanks to its simplicity, I can enjoy great health for a lifetime."

TRACEY RUSSELL, M.S., OTR/L

"After my sixth abdominal cancer surgery, I experienced problems swallowing vitamin pills and was having trouble with my digestive system. After only a few days on Living Fuel, my digestive system normalized, enabling me to eliminate ten different vitamins. Now I rely on the Seven Golden Keys and Living Fuel for my health and increased energy."

JOYCE GOMPF

SUPER HEALTH

Living
THE
SEVEN
GOLDEN
KEYS TO
LIFELONG
VITALITY
Journal

SUPER HEALTH

Living

THE
SEVEN
GOLDEN
KEYS TO
LIFELONG
VITALITY

Journal

7

KC CRAICHY

BRONZE BOW PUBLISHING

To sign up for the Super Health Newsletter
or for an overview of each of the Seven
Golden Keys as well as resources and
products related to this program,
go to www.7goldenkeys.com.

ISBN 1-932458-33-6

Published by Bronze Bow Publishing Inc.,
2600 E. 26th Street, Minneapolis, MN 55406

You can reach us on the Internet at www.bronzebowpublishing.com

Literary development and cover/interior design by Koechel Peterson & Associates, Inc., Minneapolis, Minnesota.

Manufactured in the United States of America

table of contents

FOREWORD | 11

PREFACE | 13

INTRODUCTION | 15

SEVEN GOLDEN KEYS | 17

#1—HYDRATION | 19

#2—NUTRITION | 22

#3—EXERCISE | 34

#4—STRESS | 52

#5—SLEEP | 56

#6—ENVIRONMENTAL TOXINS | 59

#7—MEDITATION AND PRAYER | 61

MY PERSONAL HISTORY | 64

MY GOALS FOR THE NEXT SEVEN WEEKS | 67

HOW TO USE THE JOURNAL | 68

SEVEN-WEEK JOURNAL | 77

CONGRATULATIONS | 189

COMPREHENSIVE NUTRITIONAL CHART | 192

FAST FOOD NUTRITIONAL CHART | 210

K.C. Craichy

Sharing a Vision for Optimal Health

A leading health advocate, author, speaker, and entrepreneur, K.C. Craichy is an authority in natural health, nutrition, and fitness. His mission is to change lives through a truly "whole person" approach to health that includes nutrition, lifestyle changes, fitness, spirituality, and much more. K.C.'s work in the area of preventative health prompted him to develop the groundbreaking nutritional approach called "The Four Corners of Optimal Nutrition," and eventually "The Seven Golden Keys to Unlock Lifelong Vitality," which form the basis for his highly acclaimed book, *Super Health*.

K.C.'s personal evolution from an overweight teenager to a health-conscious, athletic adult forged a vision within him to develop a new approach to healthy living— a simple, no-nonsense health strategy that would help people of any age and any stage of health look, feel, and live better. This became the genesis of Living Fuel, Inc., the preeminent nutrition company in the U.S. Founded in 2001, Living Fuel builds upon K.C.'s past experience of owning and operating conventional and alternative healthcare and fitness companies, as well as his passion for understanding health and his collaborative work with many of the top medical and nutritional practitioners and researchers in the United States.

K.C., his wife, Monica, and their four children live in Tampa, Florida, where his company is based. As the Founder and CEO of Living Fuel, Inc., he also shares his vision as a health consultant and speaker on the topic of Optimal Health. K.C. serves on the Clinical Nutrition Review Board (CNCB), which is the testing and certification body for the Certified Clinical Nutritionist (CCN) designation. For more information about K.C. and Living Fuel, go to www.livingfuel.com or call 1-866-580-FUEL.

foreword

K.C. Craichy is a Spirit-filled Christian with a passion to see members of the Body of Christ made whole in body, mind, and spirit. I have come to know K.C. as a sharp businessman, a diehard health enthusiast, and the leader of a godly family. But what draws me to K.C. is his undying love for Jesus and dedication to the Great Commission.

In *Super Health: The Seven Golden Keys to Unlock Lifelong Vitality,* you'll learn foundational, life-giving principles that will equip you to live the long and vibrant life your Creator intended you to live. Commonsense advice, such as the importance of daily hydration, stress reduction, and prayer, is combined with a vast amount of research that flies in the face of much conventional thinking. K.C. crushes widely held dangerous myths about health, such as the "all fat is bad" recommendation that has led to today's widespread obesity and disease.

You'll learn how to incorporate super foods, such as green juices, coconut products, chia seeds, and berries, into your daily life. You'll gain an understanding of The Four Corners of Optimal Nutrition (Calorie Restriction, Low Glycemic Foods, Healthy Fats, and High Antioxidants), and how applying them to your daily regimen can transform your health. Most importantly, you and your family will enjoy a level of health that honors God the Creator, Healer, and Sustainer.

If you just want to drop a few pounds to look better in a bathing suit, there are plenty of diets out there to try. But if you want to empower your body, mind, and spirit for an abundant purpose-filled life, I encourage you to read *Super Health.*

And remember to make today the first day of the rest of your health.

Jordan S. Rubin, N.M.D., Ph.D.
Founder of Garden of Life and *New York Times*
Best-selling Author of *The Maker's Diet*

In the late 1990s, I received a telephone phone call from K.C. Craichy, who was the CEO of a leading-edge natural health broadcast and content company at that time. As an osteopathic physician, I had been working as a full-time practitioner, while also publishing a twice-weekly Internet natural health newsletter. K.C. and I developed a friendship and mentoring relationship that continues to this day. My one-person newsletter has since transitioned into the world's most visited natural health web site. In turn, K.C.'s explorations in health innovation evolved into his highly successful company, Living Fuel, Inc.

K.C. recognized how inadequate nutrition, toxic foods, and frantic lifestyles were seriously compromising people's health. K.C.'s commitment to changing people's lives is evident in the quality of his products, which I recommend to my readers and patients, and now in his book *Super Health: The Seven Golden Keys to Unlock Lifelong Vitality*. Timely and backed by solid scientific evidence, this book truly speaks to the whole person, demonstrating the interrelatedness of hydration, nutrition, exercise, stress, sleep, environmental hazards, and meditation and prayer in overall well-being and longevity.

The information in *Super Health* is life-transforming and presented in an accessible, easy-to-understand format that will provide you with a simple, achievable, and empowering road map to a more vital life.

Dr. Joseph Mercola
New York Times Best-selling Author of the
No Grain Diet and *Total Health Cookbook*
and Founder of Mercola.com

introduction

I'm excited that you've made a commitment to improve your health through *Super Health: The Seven Golden Keys to Unlock Lifelong Vitality* program. The Seven Golden Keys are based on solid scientific principles and are the culmination of years of research and effort. Thousands of people have transformed their health through implementing these teachings into their lives.

My prayer is that this seven-week journal will help you understand better the Seven Golden Keys, which are developed comprehensively in my book *Super Health*, and how to apply them to your daily life. In these pages you will find a simple, practical, step-by-step guide to help you discover the energy, health, and fitness your body holds. It will serve as an invaluable planning, organizing, and accountability tool for your personal health.

Having reviewed numerous diets and journals over my career, I have learned that planning and recording your daily progress on the Seven Golden Keys is critical to success. Many people get started with good intentions but lack the structure and motivation to keep going. Keeping track of your accomplishments will inspire you to push harder, and it will give you confidence and a renewed sense of purpose.

Please realize that as you begin, some of the keys will be easier for you to accomplish than others. Most of our lives have a great deal of imbalance, and it takes time to restore the balance of health God wants us to enjoy. This makes it even more important that you chart your progress on each key, because each key is vital to your health. As an aid, you may want to find an accountability partner or small support group to encourage you along the way.

Whether your personal health goal is to overcome a serious health issue, to break an unhealthy habit, or to optimize your weight or athletic performance, *Super Health: Living the Seven Golden Keys to Lifelong Vitality* provides the framework for success. It will guide you day by day through the seven-week program and provide weekly summaries of progress toward your goals.

I encourage you to dive in, stay focused, and enjoy your journal as you discover the keys to optimal health!

God bless you,

K.C.

7 the seven golden keys

In *Super Health: The Seven Golden Keys to Unlock Lifelong Vitality*, you learned foundational, life-giving principles that can equip you to live the long and vibrant life your Creator intended for you. It is a true whole person approach that covers the seven major areas of your life and that have a profound impact on your health: proper hydration, nutrition, exercise, managing stress, controlling and eliminating environmental toxins, achieving restorative sleep, and meditation and prayer.

Most people excel in one or more of the Golden Keys, but few people are firing on all cylinders. Because the Golden Keys are interrelated, it is critically important to address all seven areas for physical, emotional, and spiritual renewal. For example, poor nutrition (Golden Key #2) will impact the quality of your sleep (Golden Key #5), put stress on the body (Golden Key #4), and introduce toxins into the body (Golden Key #6). And correspondingly, improvements made in any of the Golden Keys will positively affect the others. Because we are one person—mentally, physically, and spiritual—it can't be any other way. We reap what we sow on all levels of our health.

If you start with a few changes, you'll notice immediate improvements in your physical and emotional well-being. After seven weeks, you will have a new lifestyle of optimal health based on the Seven Golden Keys. This complete lifestyle program will enhance performance, promote energy, nurture overall health, and is safe and simple. You'll find yourself increasingly able to reclaim your God-given body to its fullest potential.

golden key #1

Hydration

Of all the needs of the body for health, water is by far the most important. Our body is comprised of 75 percent water, and water is involved in virtually all internal bodily reactions. It adjusts the body's temperature and rids the body of toxins. Although we can go for a month or more without food, we won't last a week without water. Yet the vast majority of us *do not get nearly enough water* to obtain optimal health and freedom from disease. We neglect our body, which is often in a chronic state of dehydration and crying out for water to fortify thirsty cells and systems. In ignoring the signs, we may be doing ourselves irreparable damage.

Another important factor is to make certain that we drink the *right* water, because most of today's water sources are contaminated and acidic (below a pH of 7.0). Making certain that the water we consume offers the greatest benefits and the least toxins is a must as we begin an active program of serious and long-term rehydration. The health benefits that we will reap from drinking the right water are enormous, because we are restoring the proper balance of water in our body—the balance upon which the enzymatic reactions and other biochemical activities within the body operate most efficiently.

From an environmental and economic perspective, the top water priority is to correct the water that comes from our taps. In *Super Health*, I recommend several water filtration systems that remove the fluoride, chlorine, other chemicals, metals, and bacteria from our water. These range from the Wellness Filter® and the Ionizer Plus® Water Micro-Filtration, which also restore the pH balance of the water, to carbon filters, such as Brita and PUR.

The vast majority of bottled waters come in plastic bottles, in spite of the fact that there is a known tendency for small amounts of the plastic in these bottles to leach out into the water itself. The safest type of bottle to drink water from is glass. But not all bottled waters are created equal...far from it. Among the hundreds of different brands of bottled water, there is a vast range in quality. Here are some products I've researched and recommend as healthy and safer bottled water choices:

- *Mountain Valley Spring Water* (glass bottle)—www.mountainvalleyspring.com
- *VOSS Artesian Water* (glass bottle)—www.vosswater.com
- *HiOsilver Oxygen Water* (glass bottle)—www.hiosilver.com
- If lead-free glass is not available, it is best to choose a bottled water that is high in pH, such as Trinity, Penta, or Fiji, as this minimizes the likeliness of leaching from the plastic.

Healthy Hydration Tips

- Sip water all day long.

- Drink water when you first get up in the morning to correct dehydration produced while you slept.

- Add a little lemon or lime juice to your water.

- Drink water at room temperature, as ice-cold water can compromise digestion.

- Limit coffee, caffeinated tea, soft drink, fruit juice, and alcohol intake.

- Use glass bottles whenever possible and never reuse plastic bottles (see Golden Key #6).

- With exercise, the American College of Sports Medicine suggests that you ensure proper hydration by beginning with a large drink of water, about 16 ounces, two hours before going out to exercise and continue during exercise.

- Discover teas—organic green, white, black, and herbal.

Getting Started—Hydration

Standard: 8 to 12 glasses of water a day.

1. Are you filtering your tap water? ____ Filter Vendor _____

2. Are you drinking bottled water out of glass or plastic? _____

3. What is the pH of the water you are drinking? _____

I highly recommend that you test your water source before and after connecting a filtration system. You can test your water's pH by purchasing a test meter at www.extech-direct.com/pH-Meters/pH-Meter-Index.htm, or you can purchase litmus paper pH test strips at your local pharmacy. You can get the overall quality of your tap water tested for free at www.mercola.com/2005/jan/15/water_filter.htm.

The Four Corners of Optimal Nutrition

While our body was designed by God to keep itself in health, the fact is that we are responsible for faithfully supplying it with absolutely all it requires for health. Twenty-four hours a day the trillions of cells in our body must be receiving the right nutrition to function at an optimal level. If we deprive our body of what it requires, or if we abuse our body with what is harmful, we will suffer a breakdown in our health. It's the simple principle of reaping what we sow.

The Four Corners of Optimal Nutrition integrate well-documented but often ignored foundations of nutrition and good health into one powerful, unified theory. Adoption of this lifestyle program can enhance performance, optimize body fat, reduce stress, and lower blood pressure, blood sugar insulin levels, cholesterol, and triglycerides.

The Four Corners of Optimal Nutrition can be likened to a team of four players. When all are used in harmony and synergy with the right balance, the results will be greater than the total of the four taken separately:

- **EATING NUTRIENT DENSE, LOW CALORIE FOODS**
  (calorie restriction—CRON) decreases free-radical damage all the way down to the mitochondria, the "power plants" or furnaces inside our cells, and thereby allows them to reproduce in a healthy fashion, protecting our energy supply and production.

- **CONSUMING LOW GLYCEMIC FOODS** ensures that we do not elevate blood sugar, which would force the release of excess insulin, promoting insulin resistance, and have the negative consequences of inflammation and fat storage.

- **ANTIOXIDANTS IN FOODS AND SUPPLEMENTS** work throughout the cells and even down into the mitochondria to protect our energy supply from free radicals.

- **A DIET RICH IN HEALTHY FATS** is essential to fuel the body and maintain cellular membrane function. This allows cells to efficiently exchange nutrients and wastes and to protect themselves from free-radical damage.

The Four Corners Nutritional Program

Finding the foods that fit into the Four Corners approach is a lot easier than you might think! Give yourself some time to become acclimated to the dietary changes that you are making and enjoy the incredible variety of health benefits that you will receive from a low calorie, low glycemic, high antioxidant, and healthy fats diet. Eating intelligently and well is a pleasure…it will not only make you feel better, but in very little time it will start to taste better too. My hope is that as you begin to implement these powerful health changes in your own life, you will begin to discover new and creative ways to enjoy the foods that will help you live longer and better.

What You Should Eat

Meet your daily macro-nutrient needs for proteins, healthy fats, and low glycemic carbohydrates through Four Corners foods, recommended meal replacements, and/or supplements. Meet your body's other daily foundational needs for enzymes, probiotics, amino acids, herbs, vitamins, minerals, antioxidants, and omega-3 EPA/DHA with the Four Corners food recommendations or recommended supplements.

- Eat a variety of salads, green vegetables, and bright-colored, above-ground vegetables. Some good choices include broccoli, spinach, kale, mixed greens, asparagus, green beans, peppers, cucumbers, barley greens, radishes, garlic, and onions.

- Eat organic, free-range eggs.

- Eat berries (cranberries, strawberries, raspberries, and blueberries).

- Eat organic chicken, turkey, grass-fed beef and lamb, and wild game, such as, venison, buffalo, and deer.

- Eat antioxidant protected fish oil and certified mercury-free Pacific salmon, summer flounder, haddock, anchovies, and sardines.

- Use virgin coconut oil, olive oil, GLA, conjugated linolenic acid (CLA), and raw organic butter.

- Use Celtic Sea Salt or Real Salt brand mineral sea salts.

Change Your Breakfast, Change Your Life

Breakfast is the meal where most people make the biggest nutritional mistakes, ranging from not eating anything to eating sugars, grains, pasteurized dairy products, pork products, or fried foods. Don't make poor breakfast choices. The goal is to get protein, healthy fats, fiber, and low glycemic carbs at *every* meal. My breakfast is always Living Fuel Rx Superfood. However, organic eggs with steamed sautéed vegetables are also an excellent choice. It is nutritionally proper to eat lunch and dinner foods for breakfast (i.e., leftover chicken or steak and salad from dinner).

The two essential reasons for eating are Foundation (building blocks) and Fuel. The third reason why people eat is for Fun. Learn how to reduce the negative impact some of these fun foods have on the human body. For instance, if you choose to consume a high starch meal, a sweet dessert, or an alcoholic beverage, you should eat high fiber foods, such as a large dark green salad or other greens, or eat quality fats and proteins beforehand, or you can get all three by Living Fuel Rx Superfood. It is helpful to drink water with lemon or have olive oil and vinegar on your salad. These help to slow the pace at which sugar enters your bloodstream, thereby reducing the harmful insulin response from the concentrated sugars.

Have a snack strategy and inventory on hand. Great snack choices are a Living Fuel Rx Super Berry™ or Super Greens smoothie, berries, salads, above-ground raw vegetables, soft-boiled eggs, raw nuts, and seeds (walnuts, almonds, macadamia nuts, Brazil nuts, CocoChia™, CocoChia Bar, coconuts, chia seeds, and pumpkin seeds).

What You Should Not Eat

The foods to avoid are the majority of foods that most people eat and by their nature are highly addictive. This part of the Four Corners approach may require some "won't power" at first. However, realize that you will be making better choices and learning new habits. Most people overcome their unhealthy cravings and food addictions to coffee, dairy, grains, and sugar after only one to four weeks.

- Minimize all grains (bread, rice, and cereal) that turn to sugar quickly; avoid all junk foods, such as French fries, anything deep fried, and pizza.

- Minimize pasteurized dairy products, such as milk, cheese, and cream.

- Minimize unfermented and genetically modified soy products.

- Minimize grain-fed, commercial beef.

- Avoid pork products and shellfish.

- Avoid farm-raised fish, such as catfish or salmon, and other fish with high mercury levels, such as tuna.

- Avoid hydrogenated oil found in commercially prepared baked goods, margarines, snacks, and processed foods.

- Minimize all sugars (candy, cookies, cakes, and syrups) and chips.

- Avoid soft drinks, sports drinks, fruit juices, sweet drinks, coffee, and alcoholic beverages.

Four Corners Shopping List

VEGETABLES
Asparagus
Avocado
Beets
Bell peppers
Broccoli
Brussels sprouts
Cabbage
Carrots
Cauliflower
Celery
Collard greens
Cucumber
Eggplant
Fennel bulb
Garlic
Green beans
Green peas
Kale
Leeks
Mustard greens
Olives
Onions
Parsley
Romaine lettuce
Root vegetables
Sea vegetables
Spinach
Squash, summer
Squash, winter
Sweet potato, with skin
Swiss chard
Tomato, fresh
Turnip greens
Yam

FISH (CERTIFIED MERCURY/PCB-FREE)
Anchovies
Fish oil plus antioxidants
Sardines

FRUITS
Apple
Apricot
Banana
Blueberries
Cantaloupe
Cranberries
Fig
Grapefruit
Grapes
Kiwi fruit
Lemons and limes
Orange
Papaya
Pear, Bartlett
Pineapple
Plum
Prune
Raisins
Raspberries
Strawberries
Watermelon

DAIRY AND EGGS
Cheeses, soft raw milk
Eggs, organic, free-range
Milk, raw goat or raw cow
Yogurt, raw goat or raw cow

BEANS AND LEGUMES
Black beans
Dried peas
Garbanzo beans

Kidney beans
Lentils
Lima beans
Miso
Navy beans
Pinto beans
Tempeh

POULTRY AND LEAN MEATS (ORGANIC)

Beef, lean, grass-fed, grain-free
Bison
Chicken, free-range
Lamb
Turkey, roast
Venison

NUTS, SEEDS, AND OILS

Almond nut butter
Almonds
Cashews
Chia seeds
Coconut
Flaxseed
Living Fuel Rx™ CocoChia™
Living Fuel Rx™ Coconut Oil
Garden of Life® Extra Virgin Coconut Oil
Macadamia nut butter
Macadamia
Olive oil
Pumpkin seeds
Valencia peanut
Walnuts

GRAIN GRASSES

Barley grass
Oat grass
Rye grass
Wheat grass

SPROUTS

Quinoa
Spelt

OTHER ACCEPTABLE GRAINS

Buckwheat
Rice, brown
Steel-cut oats

SPICES AND HERBS

Basil
Black pepper
Cayenne pepper
Chili pepper, red, dried
Cinnamon, ground
Cloves
Coriander seeds
Cumin seeds
Dill weed, dried
Ginger
Mustard seeds
Oregano
Peppermint leaves, fresh
Rosemary
Sage
Thyme, ground
Turmeric, ground

NATURAL SWEETENERS

Blackstrap molasses
Brown rice syrup
Raw Honey
Living Fuel Rx™ Therasweet™
Stevia

OTHER

Green/white/black teas
Celtic Sea Salt™ or Real Salt™
Soy sauce (tamari), organic

FOUNDATIONAL FOODS—MACRO-NUTRIENTS

Super Food Meal Replacements
Living Fuel Rx™ Super Greens
Living Fuel Rx™ Super Berry™
Garden of Life® Perfect Food®

PROTEIN SUPPLEMENTS

Living Fuel Rx™ Living Protein™
Garden of Life® Goatein (pure goat's milk protein)
IMUPlus non-denatured whey protein
RenewPro non-denatured whey protein

FOUNDATIONAL SUPPLEMENTS

Living Fuel Rx™ Omega 3&E™
Living Fuel Rx™ Pure D&A™

FOUNDATIONAL SUPPLEMENTS FOR ATHLETES AND PEOPLE OVER 40

Carnosine
CLA (congugated linololeic acid)
CoQ-10
Phosphatidylserine
Antioxidant complex
Creatine

Also, see www.makersdiet.com for other Four Corners foods and supplements.

The Glycemic Index

The Glycemic Index (GI) is just one of the many tools you have available to help improve your dietary control. It classifies foods according to how much they raise blood glucose following ingestion of an amount of the food that contains 50 grams of carbohydrates. The glycemic chart that follows is based on glucose, which is the fastest carbohydrate available except for maltose. *Glucose is given a value of 100—other carbs are given a number relative to glucose.* For the best health results, consume a diet where most of your foods have a glycemic index of less than 45.

A single serving of many high GI foods often doesn't contain 50 grams of carbohydrate. For instance, a watermelon has an extremely high GI, but one slice has so few carbohydrates that the Index is irrelevant. The Glycemic Load takes into account how many carbohydrates are actually in a serving of food you choose rather than an arbitrary serving size that contains 50 grams of carbohydrates. To calculate Glycemic Load you simply multiply the GI of a food times the number of carbohydrates in a serving of food and divide it by 100. On page 32 is a chart to show you a sample of the Glycemic Load for certain foods. A Glycemic Load of 10 or under is considered low. To learn more about GI and Glycemic Load, go to www.glycemicindex.com.

Remember, the GI is a screening tool. First, understand the GI of the food, and then ask yourself if the food is nutrient dense and healthy. For example, if ice cream has a lower GI than carrot, that does not make ice cream healthy.

Glycemic Reference List

Beans

baby lima **32**
baked **43**
black **30**
brown **38**
butter **31**
chickpeas **33**
kidney **27**
lentil **30**
navy **38**
pinto **42**
red lentils **27**
split peas **32**
soy **18**

Breads

bagel **72**
croissant **67**
kaiser roll **73**
pita **57**
pumpernickel **49**
rye **64**
rye, dark **76**
rye, whole **50**
white **72**
whole wheat **72**

Cereals

All Bran **44**
Bran Chex **58**
Cheerios **74**
Corn Bran **75**
Corn Chex **83**
Cornflakes **83**
Cream of Wheat **66**

Crispix **87**
Frosted Flakes **55**
Grapenuts **67**
Grapenuts Flakes **80**
Life **66**
Muesli **60**
NutriGrain **66**
Oatmeal **49**
Oatmeal 1 min **66**
Puffed Wheat **74**
Puffed Rice **90**
Rice Bran **19**
Rice Chex **89**
Rice Krispies **82**
Shredded Wheat **69**
Special K **54**
Swiss Muesli **60**
Total **76**

Cookies

Graham crackers **74**
oatmeal **55**
shortbread **64**
Vanilla Wafers **77**

Crackers

rice cakes **82**
rye **63**
saltine **72**
stoned wheat thins **67**
water crackers **78**

Desserts

angel food cake **67**
banana bread **47**

blueberry muffin **59**
bran muffin **60**
Danish **59**
fruit bread **47**
pound cake **54**
sponge cake **46**

Fruit

apple **38**
apricot, canned **64**
apricot, dried **30**
banana **62**
banana, unripe **30**
cantaloupe **65**
cherries **22**
dates, dried **103**
fruit cocktail **55**
grapefruit **25**
grapes **43**
kiwi **52**
mango **55**
orange **43**
papaya **58**
peach **42**
pear **36**
pineapple **66**
plum **24**
raisins **64**
strawberries **32**
strawberry jam **51**
watermelon **72**

Grains

barley **22**
brown rice **59**

buckwheat **54**
bulgur **47**
chickpeas **36**
cornmeal **68**
couscous **65**
hominy **40**
millet **75**
rice, instant **91**
rice, parboiled **47**
rye **34**
sweet corn **55**
wheat, whole **41**
white rice **88**

Juices
apple **41**
grapefruit **48**
orange **55**
pineapple **46**

Milk Products
ice cream **50**
milk **34**
pudding **43**
soy milk **31**
yogurt **38**

Pasta
brown rice pasta **92**
gnocchi **68**
linguine, durum **50**
macaroni **46**
macaroni and cheese **64**
spaghetti **40**
vermicelli **35**
vermicelli, rice **58**

Sweets
honey **58**
jelly beans **80**

Life Savers **70**
M&M's Chocolate peanuts **33**
Skittles **70**
Snickers **41**

Vegetables
beets **70**
carrots **85**
corn **70–85**
green peas **51**
green vegetables **0–15**
onions **10**
parsnips **95**
potatoes, new **58**
potatoes, russet **98**
potatoes, sweet **50**
potatoes, white **70–90**
pumpkin **75**
rutabaga **71**

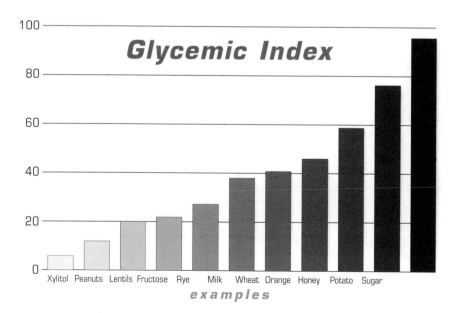

Glycemic Index

examples

The Glycemic Load

Food	GI	Serving Size	Net Carbs	GL
Peanuts	14	4 oz (113 g)	15	2
Cashew nuts	22	1 oz (30 g)	9	2
Bean sprouts	25	1 cup (104 g)	4	1
Grapefruit	25	1/2 large (166 g)	11	3
Pearled barley	25	1 cup (150 g)	42	11
Kidney beans	28	1 cup (150 g)	25	7
Pizza	30	2 slices (260 g)	42	13
Skim milk	32	8 fl oz (250 ml)	13	4
Low-fat yogurt	33	1 cup (245 g)	47	16
Spaghetti, w/wheat	37	1 cup (140 g)	37	14
Apples	38	1 medium (138 g)	16	6
Pears	38	1 medium (120 g)	11	4
All-Bran™ cereal	38	1 cup (30 g)	23	9
Rye bread	41	1 large slice (30 g)	12	5
Spaghetti	42	1 cup (140 g)	38	16
Oranges	48	1 medium (131 g)	12	6
Bananas	52	1 large (136 g)	27	14
Potato chips	54	4 oz (114 g)	55	30
Snickers Bar	55	1 bar (113 g)	64	35
Brown rice	55	1 cup (195 g)	42	23
Honey	55	1 tbsp (21 g)	17	9
Oatmeal	58	1 cup (234 g)	21	12
Ice cream	61	1 cup (72 g)	16	10
Jelly beans	78	1 oz (30 g)	28	22

Food	GI	Serving Size	Net Carbs	GL
Macaroni and cheese	64	1 serving (166 g)	47	30
Raisins	64	1 small box (43 g)	32	20
White rice	64	1 cup (186 g)	52	33
Table sugar (sucrose)	68	1 tbsp (12 g)	12	8
White bread	70	1 slice (30 g)	14	10
Watermelon	72	1 cup (154 g)	11	8
Popcorn	72	2 cups (16 g)	10	7
Soda crackers	74	4 crackers (25 g)	17	12
Doughnut	76	1 medium (47 g)	23	17
Puffed rice cakes	78	3 cakes (25 g)	21	17
Cornflakes	81	1 cup (30 g)	26	21
Baked potato	85	1 medium (173 g)	33	28
Glucose	100	(50 g)	50	50
Dates, dried	103	2 oz (60 g)	40	42

golden key #3
Exercise

Regular exercise is critically important to one's health. Studies show that exercise reduces the risk of heart attacks and strokes, improves lung and immune system function, increases mental vitality, lowers blood pressure, blood glucose, cholesterol, and triglyceride levels. Exercise can dramatically affect "secondary aging"—the incidence and severity of diseases associated with aging, such as diabetes, osteoporosis, and muscle and bone strength loss. Lifelong exercise has been shown to reduce mortality and increase life expectancy. People who exercise feel better, perform better in both work and leisure activities, and enjoy life more than people who do not exercise regularly.

Along with the proper hydration and nutrition, God has designed your body to naturally burn the fat and build muscle as you exercise it. Your body is a gift from God that keeps on giving if you treat it right. It is possible to achieve a strong, healthy, shaped body that is full of energy and vitality for a lifetime.

I know many athletes and health enthusiasts who have been very successful with their weightlifting programs for long periods of time and who are very comfortable with what they are doing. I was one of them! I also know many people who are out of shape and have been intimidated by exercise. There is a exercise program I recommend to everyone—The Seven Tiger Moves. *It is easy, fast, involves no costs, can be done anytime and anywhere, and yields maximum results.* It is the perfect answer to people's common excuses for not exercising, and it increases the dedicated weightlifter's flexibility and range of motion.

Deep Breathing Exercises

The first essential exercise is the deep breathing of pure air. Deep breathing provides: increased energy, mental alertness, and creativity, strengthened abdominal muscles, improved digestion and elimination, purified lungs, enhanced relaxation, and enhanced power throughout the entire body due to increased oxygenation of the tissues.

The secret to deep breathing is to copy the way babies breathe, using the diaphragm to create suction that pulls the air into the lungs. When the diaphragm expands and flattens, moving downward, it produces suction within the chest cavity that causes the inflow of air into the lungs. When the diaphragm relaxes and rises, air is forced out of the lungs. Both operations are of equal importance…inhalation to bring in life-giving oxygen…exhalation to expel every bit of carbon dioxide.

In the morning, while still in bed before arising, consciously relax your entire body. Inhale deeply through your nose and fill your entire lungs all the way to the maximum, hold for a count of seven seconds, then exhale slowly. During the exhale, squeeze your abdominals from the top down to the bottom (great for the abs). As you squeeze, make a "ssss" sound until you have forcefully completed your exhale. Practice this deep breathing exercise 7 to 10 times every morning. You will be amazed at your energy level.

I also recommend you do this exercise throughout the day, especially when you want to energize and recharge your thought processes or to get rid of mental or emotional stress.

Cardiovascular Exercises

Working out with the Seven Tiger Moves will result in a dramatic increase in both strength and lean muscle mass as you shed unwanted body fat. But I also recommend that you add an aerobic element to your life as well. Cardiovascular exercise is any activity that uses large muscle groups, is rhythmic in nature, and can be maintained for a period of time. Done consistently, aerobic activity trains the heart, lungs, and cardiovascular system to process and deliver oxygen in a more efficient manner.

There is walking, running, rowing, biking, swimming, elliptical training, and others to choose from. Walking is a wonderful starting point, because it is very doable, and the health benefits are marvelous. Most experts agree that 3 to 5 aerobic sessions per week for a duration of at least 20 minutes at 60 to 85 percent of your age-specific maximum heart rate is a good place to begin (see chart). You will want to do an average of 45 minutes per day, 5 or 6 days per week, and increase this by 15 to 30 minutes for maximum fat loss. You do not have to complete your exercises in a single long session. Research shows that you get the benefits of prolonged exercise sessions even when you break it up into multiple shorter sessions throughout the day.

Age	70–80% of Max Rate	60% of Max Rate
20	140–160	120
30	133–152	114
40	126–144	108
50	119–136	102
60	112–128	96
70	105–120	90

Getting Started—Exercise

Standard: 30 minutes a day, 5 to 6 times per week

1. Are you doing your deep breathing exercises each morning? _____ It only takes 10 minutes!

2. What cardiovascular exercises are you doing each week? _____ You should select at least one upper body exercise (i.e., rowing) and one lower body exercise (i.e., jogging) as part of your program.

3. Do you have a strength-training program? _____ If you don't or if you are a weightlifter, I recommend you give the Seven Tiger Moves a try. These foundational exercises will tone and strengthen your body.

The Seven Tiger Moves— Foundational Exercises

The following Isoflexion™ exercises are the Seven Tiger Moves that John Peterson learned from the legendary master of the martial arts, John McSweeney. Repetition for repetition, they deliver more benefits than virtually any other form of exercise. While they can certainly build a powerful and beautifully developed physique, as with many exercises they also help slow the aging process as well as accelerate healing.

The Seven Tiger Moves are completely natural. The secret to the system, said McSweeney, is "nothing more than contracting and extending your muscles with *great tension* while thinking into them. Tigers and lions stretch their entire body with a tension so great that their limbs actually quiver. The tiger's stretch is so powerful that it actually builds incredible strength and muscle. The inner resistance produced by the tension builds muscle fibers as much as the external resistance produced by weights or machines. However, since the resistance is perfectly controlled at all times throughout the entire range of motion, there is no jerking, no compression, and no harm to the body."

Let your body be your guide by starting your program with moderate tension and seven or more repetitions. Do additional repetitions and an additional set as you can comfortably perform them. The key to the system is the amount of tension used while performing every exercise. Vary the amount of tension until it feels comfortable. If you use only moderate tension, you will maintain muscle tone, but not dramatically increase the size of muscles. If you use higher amounts of tension, you will perform repetitions and sets as indicated in the chart below. The Seven Tiger Moves should be performed slowly with great tension. Breathe using both the nose and mouth, inhaling on the way back or up and exhaling on the way forward or down. Don't be afraid to breathe.

REPETITIONS		SETS
MODERATE	8-10	3 max
HEAVY	6-8	2-3 max
VERY HEAVY	3-5	2 max

Please read all descriptions carefully and follow the photograph sequences. You can also go to **www.7goldenkeys.com** for more information.

FULL RANGE PECTORAL CONTRACTION

PRIMARY FOCUS: CHEST

STEP 1

Stand with your left foot about a pace forward. Left knee is bent and back is straight. Hold your hands facing each other just a couple inches apart. Powerfully flex all the muscles of the arms, shoulders, chest, and upper back before movement begins.

STEP 2

Bring your hands back slowly under great tension and continue until the back muscles are fully flexed. Hold this position for a count of "one tiger one."

STEP 3

While maintaining tension in the muscles, slowly move your hands forward until they are facing each other once again just a couple inches apart. Hold this position for a count of "one tiger one," then repeat the entire sequences for 9 more repetitions.

☞ Points to Remember:

■ Be sure your arms remain parallel to the floor throughout the entire range of motion.

■ Shoulders should be held naturally and not lifted.

■ Using both your nose and mouth, breathe *in* on the way back and *out* on the way forward.

tiger move 1

SHOULDER ROLL
PRIMARY FOCUS: DELTOIDS

STEP 1

Stand with your right foot forward about one pace. Your right knee is bent and your back is straight.

STEP 2

Start with your arms bent and hands in fists. Powerfully flex all the muscles of your forearms, biceps, triceps, pectorals, and deltoids before movement begins.

STEP 3

While maintaining tension in the muscles, slowly move your arms back with your forearms remaining parallel to the floor throughout the entire range of motion until the back muscles are powerfully flexed. Hold this position for a count of "one tiger one."

STEP 4

Return to the starting position by simply reversing the motion and retracing the exact same plane of motion. Repeat the entire sequences smoothly and fluidly for 9 more repetitions.

☞ **Points to Remember:**

- Forearms remain parallel to the floor throughout the entire range of motion.

- Shoulders remain low and not lifted.

- Using both your nose and mouth, breathe *in* on the way back and *out* on the way forward.

tiger move 2

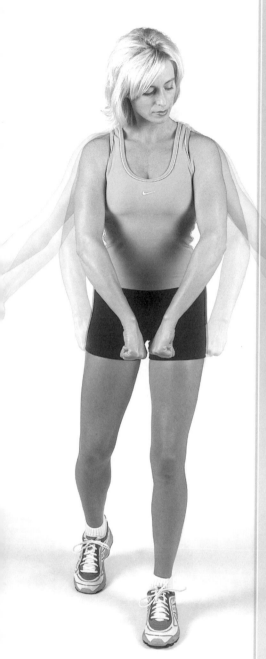

WRIST TWIST

STEP 1

Stand with your left foot one pace forward. Left knee bent, back straight, arms in front close to your body with fists turned in. Back of hands almost touching.

STEP 2

Powerfully flex the muscles of your forearms, upper arms, pectorals, and shoulders. While maintaining tension, slowly rotate your arms back, turning the fists gradually until they turn out. Flex your back muscles and triceps powerfully for a count of "one tiger one."

STEP 3

While maintaining tension slowly rotate your arms forward to starting position while turning your fists gradually until the backs of your hands are almost touching.

☞ Points to Remember:

■ Keep your arms pointing down throughout the entire range of motion.

■ This exercise works the triceps with great intensity but also works the deltoids and pectorals.

■ Keep movement smooth from beginning to end.

tiger move 3

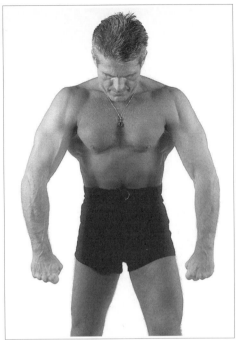

McSWEENEY HIGH REACH

STEP 1
Stand with your feet shoulder-width apart.

STEP 2
Begin with both arms at shoulder height. With your right arm slowly reach as high as possible with great tension. As your right arm comes down to your shoulder, your left arm is reaching up with great tension.

STEP 3
Continue through 10 reps with each arm.

☞ Points to Remember:

■ Arms move independently under great tension in both directions.

■ Reach as high as is comfortably possible.

■ This is the movement that John McSweeney believed to have curative powers. Many of the BronzeBowPublishing.com Forum members agree and have used it to restore full mobility to injured shoulders.

tiger move 4

ONE ARM CHIN

STEP 1

Stand with your feet side by side and shoulder-width apart. Your left arm is above your head, your right arm at shoulder level.

STEP 2

While exerting great tension in the forearms and biceps of both arms, slowly start to pull your left arm down while moving your right arm to the "up" position.

STEP 3

As each arm comes down, bring them as close to the center line of the body as possible.

☞ Points to Remember:

■ Maintaining tension in both directions.

■ Come down the center line of the body as much as possible.

■ This exercise builds and strengthens biceps, forearms, inner pectorals, and especially the latissimis dorsi of the upper back for that classic V-shape.

• • • • •

One of John Peterson's students from Boulder, Colorado, used this exercise exclusively to improve his pulling strength and went from a maximum of 4 pull-ups to 10 in just a matter of weeks. Bottom line: This is a powerful strengthener and V-builder.

tiger move 5

ABDOMINAL CONTRACTION

STEP 1

Stand with your feet side by side and shoulder-width apart. Arms in position shown, performing the Liederman chest press.

STEP 2

Press your abdomen down as hard as possible with great tension as you exhale powerfully. Hold for "one tiger one."

STEP 3

While inhaling to the maximum, consciously try to draw your abdomen in and up and try to feel as though it is touching the spine. At the point of greatest contraction, hold for "one tiger one."

☞ Points to Remember:

■ This is a great energizing exercise that can be performed anytime during the day.

■ It improves both digestion and elimination.

■ John McSweeney once told John Peterson that he had seen several people whom he knew lose several inches from their abdomens by learning how to powerfully contract both the "down" and "up" positions as indicated with this exercise.

■ This is also a great breath control exercise.

tiger move 6

HALF KNEE BEND

STEP 1

Stand with your feet side by side. Arms as shown, performing the Liederman Chest Press contraction.

STEP 2

While thinking into your leg (thigh) muscles and powerfully contracting them, slowly bend your knees and descend only halfway while maintaining maximum muscle tension.

STEP 3

Slowly reverse direction and come back up to the starting position while maintaining tension in upper body and legs.

☞ Points to Remember:

■ By maintaining an aerobic Isometric contraction of the upper body muscles (approximately 50 percent of maximum perceived effort), you will discover that it is much easier to contract the thigh muscles (quadriceps) very powerfully.

■ Breathe deeply, exhaling while going down and inhaling while coming up.

■ No need to go deeper than halfway unless you want to. But be careful not to harm the knee joint.

tiger move 7

golden key #4
Stress

Simply put, stress is synonymous with change and refers to anything that causes us to react to a physical, emotional, social, or spiritual stimulus. As we adjust to the continual fluctuations and startling threats that are a part of life, the effects can be emotional as well as physical, negative as well as positive. Anything that causes change in our lives causes stress. Even good change, such as falling in love or a promotion at work, can be stressful, but imagined change (worry and fear) can be extremely stressful. Science tells us that chronic worry and fear have devastating consequences to our health. The accumulation of stressors, whether good or bad, if intense enough, will ultimately cause physical disorders.

Stress comes in all shapes and sizes, but there are basically two kinds of stress. Bad stress (or *distress*) occurs when unresolved stress is prolonged and not dealt with in a positive way. Good stress (called *eustress*) compels us into action and results in greater awareness, emotional intelligence, and resiliency. Meeting a goal, problem solving, excelling in competition, working through a conflict with a coworker, and even grief can be important learning experiences that enrich and broaden our lives.

Without the challenges of daily life, we cannot mature and become complete human beings in a healthy way. Instead of eliminating stress, we need to learn how to *manage* it and increase our tolerance for it by following the Seven Golden Keys!

Stress Management

- **ATTITUDE AND POSITIVE SELF-TALK.** A positive attitude directly correlates with an increased ability of the immune system to fight pathogens. The ability to handle stress positively and proactively in everyday life can alleviate the constant activation of the endocrine system. And studies have shown that optimists tend to have better coping skills and to rely on more supportive social networks, which gives them a greater capacity for growth and positive reinterpretation of negative events. Stress management doesn't mean eliminating stress. It means changing how we react to it so that we don't feel overwhelmed by it. If we believe a situation is too overwhelming and we can't cope with it, that stress can damage us. There are several attitudinal modifications that can help us monitor and manage stress whenever it rears its ugly head: Acknowledge the stress, decide what you can change, gauge and monitor your emotional and physical reaction to stress, build your physical reserves, and give yourself a day of rest and relaxation.

- **EXERCISE.** The most effective techniques for fighting stress are the Seven Golden Keys, including regular and effective exercise and optimal nutrition. Exercise causes the brain to release natural endorphins, neurotransmitters in the brain that have pain-relieving properties akin to morphine. Exercise also is a detoxifier, useful in removing the byproducts of the stress response. Remember...*regular exercise* is more important than intense exercise. Working ourselves into a state of exhaustion while exercising can actually intensify feelings of anxiety, while regular, moderate exercise lowers anxiety and relaxes the body (Golden Key #3).

- **DIETARY OPTIONS AND SUPPLEMENTS.** One of the chief problems with the body's stress response has to do with the "auto-oxidation" of the very stress hormones that our body naturally release in order to help us deal with the stress. What this means is that our stress hormones *themselves* can become oxidized once they are released by our adrenal glands, which means that they then go on to create a cascade of dangerous free radicals within the body. This is one of the main reasons why chronic stress is such a killer—because of all the excess free radicals that are produced by the very release of these stress hormones. This is where antioxidants, such as full-spectrum Vitamin E and essential mineral selenium can be of tremendous help. For further recommendations on supplements, check out my book *Super Health*.

- **BREATHING AND RELAXATION.** When facing a stressful situation, relaxation and deep breathing exercises deliver immediate and direct benefits to the body, including lowering our heart rate and blood pressure and improving our sleep. Relaxation and creative visualization exercises, aromatherapy, meditation, and prayer— all of these techniques relax the mind and spirit, allowing us to feel and think better.

- **PRAYER AND MEDITATION.** Turning to God during periods of apprehension and worry is important because we learn to trust in God's power rather than ourselves. It is easy to get caught up in the materialism and egocentrism of our lives today. Spirituality gives us a broader perspective. While prayer provides a place of respite and calm during trying times, it also is an intimate conversation with God that allows us to see beyond our everyday realities and concerns, putting our stresses and anxieties into proper perspective. For more information, see Golden Key #7 in my book *Super Health*.

Getting Started—Stress

Standard: Do you feel relaxed and calm or burdened?

1. If you are feeling stressed, have you acknowledged it? _____
What can you change to help alleviate the stress? _____

_____

_____

2. Do you have a day each week for rest and relaxation? _____

3. Do you have a regular exercise program that includes deep breathing, cardiovascular, and strength training (see Golden Key #3)? _____

4. Is your diet consistent with the Four Corners of Optimal Nutrition principles? _____

5. Do you meditate and pray on a daily basis? _____

golden key #5
Sleep

Sleep is one aspect of our daily routine that many of us take for granted...until we have a couple nights in a row of either not enough sleep or interrupted sleep. It is without doubt one of the most important aspects of our daily routine as far as the maintenance of health and prevention of disease is concerned. After all, sleep is when the body regenerates itself, thereby making it ready for a whole new day of activity. Sleep gives our body a chance to rebalance itself. People who sleep well feel better, look younger, live longer, and are more energized and motivated throughout their days.

When the body is deprived of sleep, even a little bit, one's overall degree of health can easily become compromised without one even knowing it. When you wake up tired, you feel irritated through the day. Combine a lack of sleep with high stress at your job, caring for a newborn or a sick child, a heavy class load at school, or going through menopause, and we start to feel like a basket case. You can't "burn the candle at both ends" and not pay a price.

Sleep is not a luxury. It is crucial, and chronic sleep deprivation is dangerous. Sleep is an essential key to super health. Make it a priority in your life.

Natural Remedies to Help With Sleep

- Melatonin helps to make us drowsy and helps regulate sleep. Sleeping in total darkness aids in the body's natural production of melatonin, which is released by the pineal gland from within the center of the brain when one is asleep. One way that many people have found to improve their sleep is to take melatonin in supplement form.

- Create a sleep sanctuary. Make your bedroom comfortable and quiet, with beautiful drapes and pleasant, peaceful pictures. Create a place where when you enter, you immediately feel relaxed and peaceful. When you sleep, keep your bedroom completely dark to ensure maximum melatonin production. Wear ear plugs if you are easily awakened by small noises. Invest in a more comfortable bed. If it is too quiet, listen to a recording of nature sounds or soft music. Find a temperature that is most conducive to your sleeping—many people find that cool temperatures help to find a restful sleep. Don't allow the air to get stuffy. Keep the air circulating with a fan in your bedroom.

- Relax with a bath.

- Consider socks: warm feet = deep sleep.

- Supplement with GABA, which stands for gamma amino butyric acid. GABA is a natural inhibitory neurotransmitter within the brain, and it helps to induce a state of calm throughout the brain and body.

- Another terrific natural remedy for sleep disorders is the calming amino acid tryptophan. Tryptophan is now available in the U.S. without a prescription. If you have trouble getting tryptophan itself, you can get the next best thing, which is known as 5HTP.

- Embarking on the Four Corners Program for Optimal Nutrition is probably the single best step you can do to help improve the quality of your sleep.

Getting Started—Sleep

Standard: 7 to 8.5 hours

1. Are you preparing properly for sleep with a healthy diet (see Golden Key #2) and limiting fluids and caffeine prior to bedtime? _____

2. Have you created a "Sleep Sanctuary" for yourself and your family?

___ Comfortable mattress

___ Pleasant interiors (curtains, shades, lamps, pictures, rugs, pillow)

___ Climate control (air conditioning, heating, fan)

___ Lighting

___ Fragrance

___ Music

___ Ear plugs

3. If your having trouble sleeping, have you considered natural supplements, such as melatonin, GABA, or tryptophan? _____

golden key #6
Environmental Toxins

Without becoming paranoid or obsessive about environmental hazards, the reality is that we all face them everyday and in almost countless ways. Polluted air, contaminants in the water, food additives and preservatives, and pesticides and herbicides are only a few issues on an extensive list. Gradually, over time we have been exposed to steadily increasing numbers of toxic poisons, which can compromise our immune system and lead to disease. It is crucial that we educate ourselves regarding environmental hazards and effect change in our own homes to counteract and prevent them from doing their damage. It starts with keeping our immune system strong so we can deal with the constant barrage.

Given the heavy, sometimes frightening, implications of pollution and toxins, it is easy to feel helpless. The magnitude of the problem may seem overwhelming, but it is not insurmountable. We all have the capacity to affect change on a personal level. It may sound overly simple, but the first place to begin making changes is in our homes. It is important that you are aware of the environment around you, and that you make changes to the things you can control. This will give your body the best possible chance of success.

Getting Started—Environmental Hazards

Standard: Do you know the dangers? Are you taking steps to control them?

1. Have you read Golden Key #6 on Environmental Toxins in *Super Health*? That is a must read.

2. What are you storing your food and liquids in? If it is plastic, you need to consider making a change to lead-free glass for storage and ceramic or stainless steel for cookware.

3. Are you eating whole, natural organic foods whenever possible? See Golden Key #2 for the Four Corners Shopping List.

4. Have you eliminated foods with "hydrogenated" or "partially hydrogenated" oils in them?

5. Have you switched to healthier/safer brands of cosmetics/fragrances/hair products?

6. Skin Deep Report (www.ewg.org/reports/skindeep/browse_products.php)— input the brand names of cosmetics and personal care items you use and get a toxicity report.

7. Have you visited web sites that educate and provide healthy home options?

8. Learn what quality cookware, food preparation techniques, and food storage recommendations are best for your health.

9. How have you taken specific steps to minimize molds and parasites in your home?

10. How have you been tested for and minimized the impact of heavy metals in your body?

11. Are you guarded against damaging electromagnetic frequencies (EMFs) from cell phones and other electrical devices?

12. Have you improved your indoor air quality in three primary ways— eliminate sources of indoor pollution, improve ventilation, and purchase an air cleaner?

13. Have you researched immunizations and determine what is best for your family? See the following web sites and publications: *The Natural Medicine Guide to Autism* by Stephanie Marohn, www.909shot.com, www.vaccinfo.karoo.net, www.vaccineinformation.org, www.vaccination.inoz.com, defeatautistimyester-day.com, holisticmed.com/www/vaccine.html.

golden key #7
Meditation and Prayer

In today's relentless world, there is never enough time, money, or breaks from the pressures. Between juggling a career, a family, hobbies, and public duties, countless demands scream for our attention and can cause anxiety. If they reach our heart, they destroy our peace, overwhelm our emotions and minds, and can easily escalate into health problems at every level.

But in the midst of all this commotion, God is speaking to us, "Be still, and know that I am God" (Psalm 46:10). Have we stopped to listen? Can we hear Him? "How?" you may ask. Through meditation and prayer. The Lord is asking us to quiet our soul, to sit at His feet, and listen to Him. He wants to be our friend, and He wants to spend time with us.

We have seen the importance of our physical and mental health in the first six Golden Keys, which dealt primarily with the body and soul. And now we move on to the inner man, the human spirit, and meditation and prayer as the key to our spiritual health. God created you as a three-dimensional person, that is, a three-part being—you have a spirit (wisdom, consciousness, and commune), a soul (mind, will, and emotions), and a body (bone, blood, and flesh).

Meditation and prayer involves a two-part process of communicating with our Lord. Meditation prepares our spirit, soul, and body to speak and listen to God, and prayer is the act of speaking with God. What happens within our spirit has a profound affect on our whole being.

Through meditation and prayer, we take the time to get alone with Him, for only His presence will fulfill the desires of our spirit. He longs for us…waits for us to come to Him with all our heart. He knows that many of the life issues we are trying to deal with will vanish when we know Him as our heavenly Father. He wants to meet our deepest needs. But the yearning within will only be satisfied when we find God, and He cannot be found in the midst of noise and restlessness.

Meditation

Meditation is simply concentrating and focusing on several words or a single sentence on a persistent and intense basis. It incorporates and utilizes all the sensory processes, especially visualization, for an extended period of time.

Meditation and Prayer Tips

- Find a quiet, solitary place.

- Relax.

- Listen to instrumental worship music.

- Let the intrusive thoughts come and go.

- Focus on inspirational thoughts, such as "God will make a way where there is no way!"

- Visualize Jesus as the Good Shepherd to whom you go when you are distressed or frightened.

- Be comfortable physically.

- Make it a habit (establish regularity and consistency).

Prayer

Christ made it a regular priority to be alone in prayer. Do we really think we can do without it? We must have our times of being alone with our Father if we would have our heart filled with peace and our mind opened to the daily revelation that God gives to those who love Him. Make it a pattern for your life as well.

Seven Prayer Principles

1. Give thanks and praise to God.

2. Read the Bible.

3. Meditate on the Word of God.

4. Ask forgiveness for your sins and forgive others who have sinned against you.

5. Pray for others.

6. Pray for yourself.

7. Listen—meditate.

Getting Started—Meditation & Prayer

Standard: Daily

1. Have you read the chapter on Meditation and Prayer (Golden Key #7) in *Super Health*?

2. Have you found a quiet, solitary place where you can consistently meditate and pray?

3. Have you blocked out time in your daily schedule to connect with God?

My Personal History

1. Describe your general health today. _____

_____

Strengths _____

_____

Weaknesses _____

_____

2. How do you rate on the Seven Golden Keys?

☐ STANDARD ☐ POOR ☐ FAIR ☐ EXCELLENT

Hydration

8 to 12 glasses Spring Water _____

_____

Nutrition

Four Corners Program _____

_____

Exercise

Minimum 30 minutes/day, 5 or 6 times a week _____

_____

Sleep

7 to 8.5 hours a day _____

_____

Stress

Do you feel burdened or relaxed and calm?

Enviromental Toxins

Do you know the dangers? Are you taking steps to control them?

Meditation and Prayer

Excellent—daily, Poor—none

Comments

3.   Optimal Lab Values.

Prior to starting the Seven Golden Keys Program, you should consider seeing a qualified health professional to baseline your current health. For information about lab testing, go to www.totalhealthtests.com. Dr. Joseph Mercola provides panels of blood tests, with the possibility that you will be reimbursed by your insurance company. Even more importantly, the results of your blood tests will be analyzed by a computer program that does hundreds of complex analyses to give a comprehensive and individualized recommendation on how to improve your health without drugs and supplements but primarily with lifestyle changes.

Also for comprehensive lab testing, Life Extension Foundation has male and female panels. Go to lef.org for more information.

My Goals for the Next Seven Weeks

Having read the descriptions for Seven Golden Keys, what changes are you going to make to unlock lifelong vitality?

During the next 49 days, I want to improve the following:

Hydration

Nutrition

Exercise

Sleep

Stress

Environmental Toxins

Meditation and Prayer

How to Use the Daily Journal

As you look through the following journal pages, you'll note how it was organized to help you implement the Seven Golden Keys into your daily life. It was designed with efficiency in mind, requiring only a few minutes of your time each day. In the paragraphs that follow, I have filled in my own daily journal to give you an idea of how to use it.

Hydration

I recommend that you drink 8 to 12 eight-ounce glasses of mineral spring or filtered water each day. In addition to recording the amount, it is important to record the purity of the water and the quality of the container. Remember: drink out of lead-free glass whenever possible.

Nutrition

The nutrition section is divided into four areas:

1. FOUNDATION. It is critical that you understand what is required to meet your daily foundational requirements for nutrition and that you record your progress toward that standard. On a daily basis, your body needs protein, healthy fats, fiber, omega-3 (EPA/DHA), antioxidants, vitamins, minerals, probiotics, herbs, enzymes, and amino acids in order to function at an optimal level. You can meet these foundational requirements through purchasing Living Fuel Rx products (Super Berry and/or Super Greens) and Omega3&E (Antioxidant Fish Oil Caplets), or you can attempt to meet these requirements through foods and various supplementation choices. For most active people, the latter is difficult due to challenging schedules, complexity, and practicality. The advantage of using Living Fuel Rx is that it has been designed to meet your foundational requirements—all in two simple, high quality products.

Nutrition Foundation

time	source	description	X
am/pm		Protein	
am/pm		Healthy Fats	
am/pm		Fiber	
am/pm		Omega 3 EPA/DHA	
am/pm		Antioxidants	
am/pm		Vitamins	
am/pm		Minerals	
am/pm		Probiotics	
am/pm		Herbs	
am/pm		Enzymes	
am/pm		Amino Acids	

OR

time	product	description	X
8:00am am/pm	**LIVING FUEL Rx** Super Greens and/or Super Berry	Enzymes, Probiotic, Amino Acids, Herbs, Antioxidants, Vitamins and Minerals	X 2 full servings
8:00am am/pm	**LIVING FUEL Rx** Omega 3 & E	Antioxidant protected fishoil caplets. Contains Omega 3 Fatty Acidswith EPA & DHA	X 12 gelcaps

2. MEALS. It is very important that you plan your meals ahead of time. I've found that if I spend a few minutes the day or night before that I eat fresher, more nutritious foods that fit into Four Corners plan. From time to time you may want to eat "fun" foods. This is fine as long as you've had your foundational requirements, and you choose options that aren't damaging to your body, such as organic ice cream. See the Four Corners Shopping List for healthy food choices.

Meals

time	description
8:00am am/pm	Living Fuel Super Greens + Super Berry Living Fuel Super Greens + Super Berry Foundation + Fuel
11:00am am/pm	Eggs and Turkey Bacon
7:00pm am/pm	Vegetable Platter Foundation + Fuel Green Veggies – 6 servings

3. SNACKS. Having a snack inventory on hand is critical to success. Healthy snack choices include seeds (almonds, macadamia nuts, CocoChia, walnuts, Brazil nuts, pumpkin seeds), bars (CocoChia Bar), soft-boiled eggs, raw vegetables, and smoothies/shakes. Eat organic whenever possible.

Snacks			
time	product	description	comments
10:30am am/pm	CocoChia Bar	Healthy Fats	3 bars
3:00pm am/pm	Almonds	Raw	
am/pm			

4. SPECIAL SUPPLEMENTATION. For some of us, meeting our foundational requirements for nutrition is not enough. We have some special needs based on our age (over 40), occupation (athlete), or medical condition. It is important that you understand your requirements and record your special supplements as part of your overall nutritional plan.

Special Supplementation			
time	product	time	product
7:30am am/pm	CoQ 10	7:30am am/pm	Pure D+A
7:30am am/pm	Carnosine	7:30am am/pm	Antioxidant Complex
7:30am am/pm	CLA	7:30am am/pm	Phosphatidylserine

Exercise

Regular exercise is critical to one's health.

- Start the day with deep breathing exercises for 10 minutes.

- Select at least one upper and lower body cardiovascular exercise and record the time.

- A space has also been provided for you to record your strength-training program. Give the Seven Tiger Moves a try.

- You should also consider stretching a couple times per week to increase your flexibility.

Exercise			deep breathing exercises		minutes
cardio	time		strength	✓	time
Walk			7 Tiger Moves	✓	15 min.
Running	30 min.		Additional Isoflextion. See Golden Key #3 Exercise.	✓	10 min.
Biking	30 min.				
Rowing			Other High Kicks	✓	
Swimming					
Eliptical			Stretching		
Other					

Stress

In *Super Health*, you will find numerous stress management techniques. I've provided educational points for you to consider each day.

Stress

Stress is a necessary ingredient to being alive. We must learn to deal with stress in a healthy manner.

Sleep

Make certain you transform your bedroom into a sleep sanctuary. Record your bedtime and wake time. It is also important to evaluate the quality of your sleep.

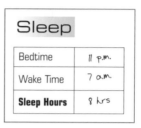

Sleep	
Bedtime	11 p.m.
Wake Time	7 a.m.
Sleep Hours	8 hrs

Environmental Toxins

This is a complex subject that requires continual learning and application. I've provided educational points for you to consider each day.

Environmental Toxins

The first and most basic part of any detoxification program is a good and balanced diet, with all of the critical nutrients that our bodies needs.

Meditation and Prayer

A daily scripture verse has been provided for you to meditate and pray over. Refer to *Super Health* to make certain you understand the fundamentals of meditation and prayer. Try to reflect on a daily verse throughout the day.

Meditation & Prayer

Beloved, I pray that in all respects you may prosper and be in good health, just as your soul prospers.—3 John 2

Commitment for Tomorrow

Purposing in your heart is critical to success. Before you go to bed, I recommend you reflect on your performance in each of the Seven Golden Keys and make a commitment for the next day. Purposing in your heart what you will do tomorrow will keep you organized and on course toward your personal health goals.

Commitment for Tomorrow:

7 Golden Keys	Commitment
Hydration	12+ Glasses of water
Nutrition	Living Fuel Rx, Veggie Plate, Poached Eggs
Exercise	45 minute run
Sleep	8 hours
Stress	Deep breathing exercises
Environmental Toxins	Aware and managing
Meditation & Prayer	Quiet time early a.m.

Week Summary

You've set standards or targets for each of the Seven Golden Keys. How are you doing versus these standards? Are you making progress in all seven areas? Over time, you should be moving from the "poor" category to "fair" and "excellent." In the "comments" section, it is important for you to record how you are feeling from a health perspective. What changes are you seeing in you body, mind and spirit? How are you doing versus your goals? And finally, you must plan for next week. What areas do you need to most improve in? Set specific goals for these areas.

week 1 summary

date: **April 26**

7 Golden Keys	Standard	Poor	Fair	Excellent
Hydration	8–12 glasses Spring Water			X
Nutrition	Four Corners Program			X
Exercise	Minimum 30 minutes/day, 5–6 times/week			X
Sleep	7–8.5 hours/day		X	
Stress	Do you feel burdened or relaxed & calm? Excellent—calm, Poor—burdened		X	
Environmental Toxins	Do you know the dangers & are you taking steps in your control?			X
Meditation & Prayer	Excellent—daily, Poor—none		X	

Comments:

This week was filled with numerous deadlines at work
and a TV show appearance. I did not sleep as well
as I normally do and at times I felt stressed.
Daily exercise, prayer and proper nutrition carried
me through the week.

Commitment for Next Week:

Stay on the 7 Golden Keys program while traveling
early in the week. Seek improvement in sleep quality
and expand meditation + prayer time.

 **day 1**

date: _____

Hydration 8 oz. glasses of spring water

 (1) (2) (3) (4) (5) (6) (7) (8) (9) (10) (11) (12)

Nutrition Foundation

time	source	description	X
am/pm		Protein	
am/pm		Healthy Fats	
am/pm		Fiber	
am/pm		Omega 3 EPA/DHA	
am/pm		Antioxidants	
am/pm		Vitamins	
am/pm		Minerals	
am/pm		Probiotics	
am/pm		Herbs	
am/pm		Enzymes	
am/pm		Amino Acids	

OR

time	product	description	X
am/pm	**LIVING FUEL Rx** Super Greens and/or Super Berry	Enzymes, Probiotic, Amino Acids, Herbs, Antioxidants, Vitamins and Minerals	
am/pm	**LIVING FUEL Rx** Omega 3 & E	Antioxidant protected fish oil caplets. Contains Omega 3 Fatty Acids with EPA & DHA	

Vegetables (Super Health Shopping List)

1	2	3	4	5	6	7	8

Fruits

1	2	3

Meals

time	description
am/pm	
am/pm	
am/pm	

Snacks

time	product	description	comments
am/pm			
am/pm			
am/pm			

Special Supplementation

time	product	time	product
am/pm		am/pm	
am/pm		am/pm	
am/pm		am/pm	

Exercise

cardio	time
Walking	
Running	
Biking	
Rowing	
Swimming	
Elliptical	
Other	

deep breathing exercises	minutes

strength	✓	time
7 Tiger Moves		
Additional Isoflexion. See Golden Key #3 Exercise.		
Other		
Stretching		

Stress

How we handle stress has a major impact on our health.

Sleep

Bedtime	
Wake Time	
Sleep Hours	

Environmental Toxins

Gradually, over time we have been exposed to steadily increasing numbers of toxic poisons, which can lead to disease.

Meditation & Prayer

Sing to Him, sing psalms to Him; talk of all His wondrous works! Glory in His holy name; let the hearts of those rejoice who seek the LORD! Seek the LORD and His strength; seek His face evermore!—Psalm 105:2–4

Commitment for Tomorrow:

7 Golden Keys	Commitment
Hydration	
Nutrition	
Exercise	
Sleep	
Stress	
Environmental Toxins	
Meditation & Prayer	

 **day 2**

date: _____

Hydration 8 oz. glasses of spring water

(1) (2) (3) (4) (5) (6) (7) (8) (9) (10) (11) (12)

Nutrition Foundation

time	source	description	X
am/pm		Protein	
am/pm		Healthy Fats	
am/pm		Fiber	
am/pm		Omega 3 EPA/DHA	
am/pm		Antioxidants	
am/pm		Vitamins	
am/pm		Minerals	
am/pm		Probiotics	
am/pm		Herbs	
am/pm		Enzymes	
am/pm		Amino Acids	

OR

time	product	description	X
am/pm	**LIVING FUEL Rx** Super Greens and/or Super Berry	Enzymes, Probiotic, Amino Acids, Herbs, Antioxidants, Vitamins and Minerals	
am/pm	**LIVING FUEL Rx** Omega 3 & E	Antioxidant protected fish oil caplets. Contains Omega 3 Fatty Acids with EPA & DHA	

Vegetables (Super Health Shopping List)

1	2	3	4	5	6	7	8

Fruits

1	2	3

Meals

time	description
am/pm	
am/pm	
am/pm	

Snacks

time	product	description	comments
am/pm			
am/pm			
am/pm			

Special Supplementation

time	product	time	product
am/pm		am/pm	
am/pm		am/pm	
am/pm		am/pm	

Exercise

deep breathing exercises		minutes

cardio	time
Walk	
Running	
Biking	
Rowing	
Swimming	
Elliptical	
Other	

strength	✓	time
7 Tiger Moves		
Additional Isoflexion. See Golden Key #3 Exercise.		
Other		
Stretching		

Stress

Stress is synonymous with change and refers to anything that causes us to react to a physical, mental, emotional, social, or spiritual stimulus.

Sleep

Bedtime	
Wake Time	
Sleep Hours	

Environmental Toxins

We are under attack from unseen hazards, and this is magnified by a poor diet and lifestyle choices.

Meditation & Prayer

"And whenever you stand praying, if you have anything against anyone, forgive him, that your Father in heaven may also forgive you your trespasses."
—Mark 11:25

Commitment for Tomorrow:

7 Golden Keys	Commitment
Hydration	
Nutrition	
Exercise	
Sleep	
Stress	
Environmental Toxins	
Meditation & Prayer	

day 3

date: _____

Hydration 8 oz. glasses of spring water

(1) (2) (3) (4) (5) (6) (7) (8) (9) (10) (11) (12)

Nutrition Foundation

time	source	description	X
am/pm		Protein	
am/pm		Healthy Fats	
am/pm		Fiber	
am/pm		Omega 3 EPA/DHA	
am/pm		Antioxidants	
am/pm		Vitamins	
am/pm		Minerals	
am/pm		Probiotics	
am/pm		Herbs	
am/pm		Enzymes	
am/pm		Amino Acids	

OR

time	product	description	X
am/pm	**LIVING FUEL Rx** Super Greens and/or Super Berry	Enzymes, Probiotic, Amino Acids, Herbs, Antioxidants, Vitamins and Minerals	
am/pm	**LIVING FUEL Rx** Omega 3 & E	Antioxidant protected fish oil caplets. Contains Omega 3 Fatty Acids with EPA & DHA	

Vegetables (Super Health Shopping List)

1	2	3	4	5	6	7	8

Fruits

1	2	3

Meals

time	description
am/pm	
am/pm	
am/pm	

Snacks

time	product	description	comments
am/pm			
am/pm			
am/pm			

Special Supplementation

time	product	time	product
am/pm		am/pm	
am/pm		am/pm	
am/pm		am/pm	

Exercise

cardio	time
Walk	
Running	
Biking	
Rowing	
Swimming	
Elliptical	
Other	

deep breathing exercises		minutes
strength	✓	time
7 Tiger Moves		
Additional Isoflexion. See Golden Key #3 Exercise.		
Other		
Stretching		

Stress

Even good change can be stressful, but imagined change (worry and fear) can be extremely stressful.

Sleep

Bedtime	
Wake Time	
Sleep Hours	

Environmental Toxins

While we can enjoy and benefit from the bounty all around us, we also have a responsibility to uphold and protect it.

Meditation & Prayer

If we confess our sins, He is faithful and just to forgive us our sins and to cleanse us from all unrighteousness.—1 John 1:9

Commitment for Tomorrow:

7 Golden Keys	Commitment
Hydration	
Nutrition	
Exercise	
Sleep	
Stress	
Environmental Toxins	
Meditation & Prayer	

 **day 4**

date: _____

Hydration 8 oz. glasses of spring water

 1　 2　3　 4　5　 6　7　 8　9　 10　11　12

Nutrition Foundation

time	source	description	X
am/pm		Protein	
am/pm		Healthy Fats	
am/pm		Fiber	
am/pm		Omega 3 EPA/DHA	
am/pm		Antioxidants	
am/pm		Vitamins	
am/pm		Minerals	
am/pm		Probiotics	
am/pm		Herbs	
am/pm		Enzymes	
am/pm		Amino Acids	

OR

time	product	description	X
am/pm	**LIVING FUEL Rx** Super Greens and/or Super Berry	Enzymes, Probiotic, Amino Acids, Herbs, Antioxidants, Vitamins and Minerals	
am/pm	**LIVING FUEL Rx** Omega 3 & E	Antioxidant protected fish oil caplets. Contains Omega 3 Fatty Acids with EPA & DHA	

Vegetables (Super Health Shopping List)

1	2	3	4	5	6	7	8

Fruits

1	2	3

Meals

time	description
am/pm	
am/pm	
am/pm	

Snacks

time	product	description	comments
am/pm			
am/pm			
am/pm			

Special Supplementation

time	product	time	product
am/pm		am/pm	
am/pm		am/pm	
am/pm		am/pm	

Exercise

cardio	time
Walk	
Running	
Biking	
Rowing	
Swimming	
Elliptical	
Other	

deep breathing exercises	minutes

strength	✓	time
7 Tiger Moves		
Additional Isoflexion. See Golden Key #3 Exercise.		
Other		
Stretching		

Stress

Chronic worry and fear can have dramatic consequences on our health.

Sleep

Bedtime	
Wake Time	
Sleep Hours	

Environmental Toxins

The bottom line is that we must take control of what is controllable and help our bodies withstand the constant attacks from sources we cannot control.

Meditation & Prayer

Now in the morning, having risen a long while before daylight, He went out and departed to a solitary place; and there He prayed.—Mark 1:35

Commitment for Tomorrow:

7 Golden Keys	Commitment
Hydration	
Nutrition	
Exercise	
Sleep	
Stress	
Environmental Toxins	
Meditation & Prayer	

 **day 5**

date: _____

Hydration 8 oz. glasses of spring water

 (1) (2) (3) (4) (5) (6) (7) (8) (9) (10) (11) (12)

Nutrition Foundation

time	source	description	X
am/pm		Protein	
am/pm		Healthy Fats	
am/pm		Fiber	
am/pm		Omega 3 EPA/DHA	
am/pm		Antioxidants	
am/pm		Vitamins	
am/pm		Minerals	
am/pm		Probiotics	
am/pm		Herbs	
am/pm		Enzymes	
am/pm		Amino Acids	

OR

time	product	description	X
am/pm	**LIVING FUEL Rx** Super Greens and/or Super Berry	Enzymes, Probiotic, Amino Acids, Herbs, Antioxidants, Vitamins and Minerals	
am/pm	**LIVING FUEL Rx** Omega 3 & E	Antioxidant protected fish oil caplets. Contains Omega 3 Fatty Acids with EPA & DHA	

Vegetables (Super Health Shopping List)

1	2	3	4	5	6	7	8

Fruits

1	2	3

Meals

time	description
am/pm	
am/pm	
am/pm	

Snacks

time	product	description	comments
am/pm			
am/pm			
am/pm			

Special Supplementation

time	product	time	product
am/pm		am/pm	
am/pm		am/pm	
am/pm		am/pm	

Exercise

cardio	time
Walk	
Running	
Biking	
Rowing	
Swimming	
Elliptical	
Other	

deep breathing exercises		minutes

strength	✓	time
7 Tiger Moves		
Additional Isoflexion. See Golden Key #3 Exercise.		
Other		
Stretching		

Stress

The body has its own natural ability for preventing disease and dealing with stress.

Sleep

Bedtime	
Wake Time	
Sleep Hours	

Environmental Toxins

Troubles began with the introduction of large quantities of pesticides into our environment in the 1930s to protect agricultural crops.

Meditation & Prayer

Bless the LORD, O my soul, and forget not all His benefits: who forgives all your iniquities, who heals all your diseases, who redeems your life from destruction, who crowns you with loving kindness and tender mercies, who satisfies your mouth with good things, so that your youth is renewed like the eagle's.—Psalm 103:2–5

Commitment for Tomorrow:

7 Golden Keys	Commitment
Hydration	
Nutrition	
Exercise	
Sleep	
Stress	
Environmental Toxins	
Meditation & Prayer	

day 6

*date:*_____

Hydration 8 oz. glasses of spring water

(1) (2) (3) (4) (5) (6) (7) (8) (9) (10) (11) (12)

Nutrition Foundation

time	source	description	X
am/pm		Protein	
am/pm		Healthy Fats	
am/pm		Fiber	
am/pm		Omega 3 EPA/DHA	
am/pm		Antioxidants	
am/pm		Vitamins	
am/pm		Minerals	
am/pm		Probiotics	
am/pm		Herbs	
am/pm		Enzymes	
am/pm		Amino Acids	

OR

time	product	description	X
am/pm	**LIVING FUEL Rx** Super Greens and/or Super Berry	Enzymes, Probiotic, Amino Acids, Herbs, Antioxidants, Vitamins and Minerals	
am/pm	**LIVING FUEL Rx** Omega 3 & E	Antioxidant protected fish oil caplets. Contains Omega 3 Fatty Acids with EPA & DHA	

Vegetables (Super Health Shopping List)

1	2	3	4	5	6	7	8

Fruits

1	2	3

Meals

time	description
am/pm	
am/pm	
am/pm	

Snacks

time	product	description	comments
am/pm			
am/pm			
am/pm			

Special Supplementation

time	product	time	product
am/pm		am/pm	
am/pm		am/pm	
am/pm		am/pm	

Exercise

cardio	time
Walk	
Running	
Biking	
Rowing	
Swimming	
Elliptical	
Other	

deep breathing exercises		minutes
strength	✓	time
7 Tiger Moves		
Additional Isoflexion. See Golden Key #3 Exercise.		
Other		
Stretching		

Stress

"A stress-free life is an impossible goal—we need some stress to be alive. After all, we call it blood pressure. Without some pressure, we are dead."—Dr. Hans Selye

Sleep

Bedtime	
Wake Time	
Sleep Hours	

Environmental Toxins

There are approximately 77,000 chemicals produced in North America agriculture alone.

Meditation & Prayer

"But I say to you, love your enemies, bless those who curse you, do good to those who hate you, and pray for those who spitefully use you and persecute you."—Matthew 5:44

Commitment for Tomorrow:

7 Golden Keys	Commitment
Hydration	
Nutrition	
Exercise	
Sleep	
Stress	
Environmental Toxins	
Meditation & Prayer	

 **day 7**

date: _____

Hydration 8 oz. glasses of spring water

(1) (2) (3) (4) (5) (6) (7) (8) (9) (10) (11) (12)

Nutrition Foundation

time	source	description	X
am/pm		Protein	
am/pm		Healthy Fats	
am/pm		Fiber	
am/pm		Omega 3 EPA/DHA	
am/pm		Antioxidants	
am/pm		Vitamins	
am/pm		Minerals	
am/pm		Probiotics	
am/pm		Herbs	
am/pm		Enzymes	
am/pm		Amino Acids	

OR

time	product	description	X
am/pm	**LIVING FUEL Rx** Super Greens and/or Super Berry	Enzymes, Probiotic, Amino Acids, Herbs, Antioxidants, Vitamins and Minerals	
am/pm	**LIVING FUEL Rx** Omega 3 & E	Antioxidant protected fish oil caplets. Contains Omega 3 Fatty Acids with EPA & DHA	

Vegetables (Super Health Shopping List)

1	2	3	4	5	6	7	8

Fruits

1	2	3

Meals

time	description
am/pm	
am/pm	
am/pm	

Snacks

time	product	description	comments
am/pm			
am/pm			
am/pm			

Special Supplementation

time	product	time	product
am/pm		am/pm	
am/pm		am/pm	
am/pm		am/pm	

Exercise

deep breathing exercises		minutes

cardio	time
Walk	
Running	
Biking	
Rowing	
Swimming	
Elliptical	
Other	

strength	✓	time
7 Tiger Moves		
Additional Isoflexion. See Golden Key #3 Exercise.		
Other		
Stretching		

Stress

If stress becomes chronic and long-term, which it does in many of our lives, our feedback loops become degraded, and we experience adrenal fatigue.

Sleep

Bedtime	
Wake Time	
Sleep Hours	

Environmental Toxins

There are 1,000 new chemicals introduced each year.

Meditation & Prayer

"If My people who are called by My name will humble themselves, and pray and seek My face, and turn from their wicked ways, then I will hear from heaven, and will forgive their sin and heal their land."—2 Chronicles 7:14

Commitment for Tomorrow:

7 Golden Keys	Commitment
Hydration	
Nutrition	
Exercise	
Sleep	
Stress	
Environmental Toxins	
Meditation & Prayer	

week 1 summary

date: _____

7 Golden Keys	Standard	Poor	Fair	Excellent
Hydration	8–12 glasses Spring Water			
Nutrition	Four Corners Program			
Exercise	Minimum 30 minutes/day, 5–6 times/week			
Sleep	7–8.5 hours/day			
Stress	Do you feel burdened or relaxed & calm? Excellent—calm, Poor—burdened			
Environmental Toxins	Do you know the dangers & are you taking steps in your control?			
Meditation & Prayer	Excellent—daily, Poor—none			

Comments:

Commitment for Next Week:

week 1

 **day 8**

date: _____

Hydration   8 oz. glasses of spring water

(1) (2) (3) (4) (5) (6) (7) (8) (9) (10) (11) (12)

Nutrition   Foundation

time	source	description	X
am/pm		Protein	
am/pm		Healthy Fats	
am/pm		Fiber	
am/pm		Omega 3 EPA/DHA	
am/pm		Antioxidants	
am/pm		Vitamins	
am/pm		Minerals	
am/pm		Probiotics	
am/pm		Herbs	
am/pm		Enzymes	
am/pm		Amino Acids	

OR

time	product	description	X
am/pm	**LIVING FUEL Rx** Super Greens and/or Super Berry	Enzymes, Probiotic, Amino Acids, Herbs, Antioxidants, Vitamins and Minerals	
am/pm	**LIVING FUEL Rx** Omega 3 & E	Antioxidant protected fish oil caplets. Contains Omega 3 Fatty Acids with EPA & DHA	

Vegetables (Super Health Shopping List)

1	2	3	4	5	6	7	8

Fruits

1	2	3

Meals

time	description
am/pm	
am/pm	
am/pm	

Snacks

time	product	description	comments
am/pm			
am/pm			
am/pm			

Special Supplementation

time	product	time	product
am/pm		am/pm	
am/pm		am/pm	
am/pm		am/pm	

Exercise

	deep breathing exercises		minutes

cardio	time
Walk	
Running	
Biking	
Rowing	
Swimming	
Elliptical	
Other	

strength	✓	time
7 Tiger Moves		
Additional Isoflexion. See Golden Key #3 Exercise.		
Other		
Stretching		

Stress

Our response to stress when it occurs determines how the stress will affect us.

Sleep

Bedtime	
Wake Time	
Sleep Hours	

Environmental Toxins

Change in farming methods has led to a decline in the quality and nutritious content of our foods.

Meditation & Prayer

"I am the vine, you are the branches. He who abides in Me, and I in him, bears much fruit; for without Me you can do nothing."—John 15:5

Commitment for Tomorrow:

7 Golden Keys	Commitment
Hydration	
Nutrition	
Exercise	
Sleep	
Stress	
Environmental Toxins	
Meditation & Prayer	

 **day 9**

date: _____

Hydration   8 oz. glasses of spring water

(1) (2) (3) (4) (5) (6) (7) (8) (9) (10) (11) (12)

Nutrition   Foundation

time	source	description	X
am/pm		Protein	
am/pm		Healthy Fats	
am/pm		Fiber	
am/pm		Omega 3 EPA/DHA	
am/pm		Antioxidants	
am/pm		Vitamins	
am/pm		Minerals	
am/pm		Probiotics	
am/pm		Herbs	
am/pm		Enzymes	
am/pm		Amino Acids	

OR

time	product	description	X
am/pm	**LIVING FUEL Rx** Super Greens and/or Super Berry	Enzymes, Probiotic, Amino Acids, Herbs, Antioxidants, Vitamins and Minerals	
am/pm	**LIVING FUEL Rx** Omega 3 & E	Antioxidant protected fish oil caplets. Contains Omega 3 Fatty Acids with EPA & DHA	

Vegetables (Super Health Shopping List)

1	2	3	4	5	6	7	8

Fruits

1	2	3

Meals

time	description
am/pm	
am/pm	
am/pm	

Snacks

time	product	description	comments
am/pm			
am/pm			
am/pm			

Special Supplementation

time	product	time	product
am/pm		am/pm	
am/pm		am/pm	
am/pm		am/pm	

Exercise

cardio	time
Walk	
Running	
Biking	
Rowing	
Swimming	
Elliptical	
Other	

deep breathing exercises		minutes
strength	✓	time
7 Tiger Moves		
Additional Isoflexion. See Golden Key #3 Exercise.		
Other		
Stretching		

Stress

The accumulation of stressors, whether good or bad, if intense enough, will ultimately cause physical disorders.

Sleep

Bedtime	
Wake Time	
Sleep Hours	

Environmental Toxins

Farming methods changed drastically when farmers switched from organic to synthetic products, leading to weakened immune systems.

Meditation & Prayer

Enter into His gates with thanksgiving, and into His courts with praise. Be thankful to Him, and bless His name.—Psalm 100:4

Commitment for Tomorrow:

7 Golden Keys	Commitment
Hydration	
Nutrition	
Exercise	
Sleep	
Stress	
Environmental Toxins	
Meditation & Prayer	

 day 10

date: _____

Hydration 8 oz. glasses of spring water

(1) (2) (3) (4) (5) (6) (7) (8) (9) (10) (11) (12)

Nutrition Foundation

time	source	description	X
am/pm		Protein	
am/pm		Healthy Fats	
am/pm		Fiber	
am/pm		Omega 3 EPA/DHA	
am/pm		Antioxidants	
am/pm		Vitamins	
am/pm		Minerals	
am/pm		Probiotics	
am/pm		Herbs	
am/pm		Enzymes	
am/pm		Amino Acids	

OR

time	product	description	X
am/pm	**LIVING FUEL Rx** Super Greens and/or Super Berry	Enzymes, Probiotic, Amino Acids, Herbs, Antioxidants, Vitamins and Minerals	
am/pm	**LIVING FUEL Rx** Omega 3 & E	Antioxidant protected fish oil caplets. Contains Omega 3 Fatty Acids with EPA & DHA	

Vegetables (Super Health Shopping List)

1	2	3	4	5	6	7	8

Fruits

1	2	3

Meals

time	description
am/pm	
am/pm	
am/pm	

Snacks

time	product	description	comments
am/pm			
am/pm			
am/pm			

Special Supplementation

time	product	time	product
am/pm		am/pm	
am/pm		am/pm	
am/pm		am/pm	

Exercise

deep breathing exercises		minutes

cardio	time
Walk	
Running	
Biking	
Rowing	
Swimming	
Elliptical	
Other	

strength	✓	time
7 Tiger Moves		
Additional Isoflexion. See Golden Key #3 Exercise.		
Other		
Stretching		

Stress

It is not that stress is harmful—it is *dis*tress that is harmful. Distress occurs when unresolved emotional stress is prolonged and not dealt with in a positive way.

Sleep

Bedtime	
Wake Time	
Sleep Hours	

Environmental Toxins

The massive use of chemical fertilizers and pesticides changed the whole fabric of agriculture and farming.

Meditation & Prayer

And you will seek Me and find Me, when you search for Me with all your heart.—Jeremiah 29:13

Commitment for Tomorrow:

7 Golden Keys	Commitment
Hydration	
Nutrition	
Exercise	
Sleep	
Stress	
Environmental Toxins	
Meditation & Prayer	

day 10

day 11

date: _____

Hydration 8 oz. glasses of spring water

   (4) (5)   (8) (9)

(1) (2) (3) (4) (5) (6) (7) (8) (9) (10) (11) (12)

Nutrition Foundation

time	source	description	X
am/pm		Protein	
am/pm		Healthy Fats	
am/pm		Fiber	
am/pm		Omega 3 EPA/DHA	
am/pm		Antioxidants	
am/pm		Vitamins	
am/pm		Minerals	
am/pm		Probiotics	
am/pm		Herbs	
am/pm		Enzymes	
am/pm		Amino Acids	

OR

time	product	description	X
am/pm	**LIVING FUEL Rx** Super Greens and/or Super Berry	Enzymes, Probiotic, Amino Acids, Herbs, Antioxidants, Vitamins and Minerals	
am/pm	**LIVING FUEL Rx** Omega 3 & E	Antioxidant protected fish oil caplets. Contains Omega 3 Fatty Acids with EPA & DHA	

Vegetables (Super Health Shopping List)

1	2	3	4	5	6	7	8

Fruits

1	2	3

Meals

time	description
am/pm	
am/pm	
am/pm	

Snacks

time	product	description	comments
am/pm			
am/pm			
am/pm			

Special Supplementation

time	product	time	product
am/pm		am/pm	
am/pm		am/pm	
am/pm		am/pm	

Exercise

cardio	time
Walk	
Running	
Biking	
Rowing	
Swimming	
Elliptical	
Other	

deep breathing exercises		minutes

strength	✓	time
7 Tiger Moves		
Additional Isoflexion. See Golden Key #3 Exercise.		
Other		
Stretching		

Stress

Some physicians estimate that stress and anxiety may be a contributing factor in 90 percent of illnesses.

Sleep

Bedtime	
Wake Time	
Sleep Hours	

Environmental Toxins

Take control and bring change to what you allow in your own home.

Meditation & Prayer

"But you, when you pray, go into your room, and when you have shut your door, pray to your Father who is in the secret place; and your Father who sees in secret will reward you openly."—Matthew 6:6

Commitment for Tomorrow:

7 Golden Keys	Commitment
Hydration	
Nutrition	
Exercise	
Sleep	
Stress	
Environmental Toxins	
Meditation & Prayer	

 **day 12**

date: _____

Hydration 8 oz. glasses of spring water

(1) (2) (3) (4) (5) (6) (7) (8) (9) (10) (11) (12)

Nutrition Foundation

time	source	description	X
am/pm		Protein	
am/pm		Healthy Fats	
am/pm		Fiber	
am/pm		Omega 3 EPA/DHA	
am/pm		Antioxidants	
am/pm		Vitamins	
am/pm		Minerals	
am/pm		Probiotics	
am/pm		Herbs	
am/pm		Enzymes	
am/pm		Amino Acids	

OR

time	product	description	X
am/pm	**LIVING FUEL Rx** Super Greens and/or Super Berry	Enzymes, Probiotic, Amino Acids, Herbs, Antioxidants, Vitamins and Minerals	
am/pm	**LIVING FUEL Rx** Omega 3 & E	Antioxidant protected fish oil caplets. Contains Omega 3 Fatty Acids with EPA & DHA	

Vegetables (Super Health Shopping List)

1	2	3	4	5	6	7	8

Fruits

1	2	3

Meals

time	description
am/pm	
am/pm	
am/pm	

Snacks

time	product	description	comments
am/pm			
am/pm			
am/pm			

Special Supplementation

time	product	time	product
am/pm		am/pm	
am/pm		am/pm	
am/pm		am/pm	

Exercise

cardio	time
Walk	
Running	
Biking	
Rowing	
Swimming	
Elliptical	
Other	

deep breathing exercises	minutes

strength	✓	time
7 Tiger Moves		
Additional Isoflexion. See Golden Key #3 Exercise.		
Other		
Stretching		

Stress

Good stress compels us into action and results in greater awareness, emotional intelligence, and resiliency.

Sleep

Bedtime	
Wake Time	
Sleep Hours	

Environmental Toxins

Most toxins are fat-soluble poisons that have been accumulating and persisting in our own fat tissue.

Meditation & Prayer

Be anxious for nothing, but in everything by prayer and supplication, with thanksgiving, let your requests be made known to God.—Philippians 4:6

Commitment for Tomorrow:

7 Golden Keys	Commitment
Hydration	
Nutrition	
Exercise	
Sleep	
Stress	
Environmental Toxins	
Meditation & Prayer	

day 12

 **day 13**

date: _____

Hydration 8 oz. glasses of spring water

 (1) (2) (3) (4) (5) (6) (7) (8) (9) (10) (11) (12)

Nutrition Foundation

time	source	description	X
am/pm		Protein	
am/pm		Healthy Fats	
am/pm		Fiber	
am/pm		Omega 3 EPA/DHA	
am/pm		Antioxidants	
am/pm		Vitamins	
am/pm		Minerals	
am/pm		Probiotics	
am/pm		Herbs	
am/pm		Enzymes	
am/pm		Amino Acids	

OR

time	product	description	X
am/pm	**LIVING FUEL Rx** Super Greens and/or Super Berry	Enzymes, Probiotic, Amino Acids, Herbs, Antioxidants, Vitamins and Minerals	
am/pm	**LIVING FUEL Rx** Omega 3 & E	Antioxidant protected fish oil caplets. Contains Omega 3 Fatty Acids with EPA & DHA	

Vegetables (Super Health Shopping List)

1	2	3	4	5	6	7	8

Fruits

1	2	3

Meals

time	description
am/pm	
am/pm	
am/pm	

Snacks

time	product	description	comments
am/pm			
am/pm			
am/pm			

Special Supplementation

time	product	time	product
am/pm		am/pm	
am/pm		am/pm	
am/pm		am/pm	

Exercise

cardio	time
Walk	
Running	
Biking	
Rowing	
Swimming	
Elliptical	
Other	

deep breathing exercises	minutes

strength	✓	time
7 Tiger Moves		
Additional Isoflexion. See Golden Key #3 Exercise.		
Other		
Stretching		

Stress

Instead of eliminating stress, we need to learn to manage it and increase our tolerance for it.

Sleep

Bedtime	
Wake Time	
Sleep Hours	

Environmental Toxins

Breast milk is still the healthiest food for infants.

Meditation & Prayer

And when they had prayed, the place where they were assembled together was shaken; and they were all filled with the Holy Spirit, and they spoke the word of God with boldness.—Acts 4:31

Commitment for Tomorrow:

7 Golden Keys	Commitment
Hydration	
Nutrition	
Exercise	
Sleep	
Stress	
Environmental Toxins	
Meditation & Prayer	

day 13

 **day 14**   *date:* _____

Hydration   8 oz. glasses of spring water

 (1) (2) (3) (4) (5) (6) (7) (8) (9) (10) (11) (12)

Nutrition Foundation

time	source	description	X
am/pm		Protein	
am/pm		Healthy Fats	
am/pm		Fiber	
am/pm		Omega 3 EPA/DHA	
am/pm		Antioxidants	
am/pm		Vitamins	
am/pm		Minerals	
am/pm		Probiotics	
am/pm		Herbs	
am/pm		Enzymes	
am/pm		Amino Acids	

OR

time	product	description	X
am/pm	**LIVING FUEL Rx** Super Greens and/or Super Berry	Enzymes, Probiotic, Amino Acids, Herbs, Antioxidants, Vitamins and Minerals	
am/pm	**LIVING FUEL Rx** Omega 3 & E	Antioxidant protected fish oil caplets. Contains Omega 3 Fatty Acids with EPA & DHA	

Vegetables (Super Health Shopping List)

1	2	3	4	5	6	7	8

Fruits

1	2	3

Meals

time	description
am/pm	
am/pm	
am/pm	

Snacks

time	product	description	comments
am/pm			
am/pm			
am/pm			

Special Supplementation

time	product	time	product
am/pm		am/pm	
am/pm		am/pm	
am/pm		am/pm	

Exercise

cardio	time
Walk	
Running	
Biking	
Rowing	
Swimming	
Elliptical	
Other	

deep breathing exercises		minutes

strength	✓	time
7 Tiger Moves		
Additional Isoflexion. See Golden Key #3 Exercise.		
Other		
Stretching		

Stress

Stress management can help lower blood sugar as well as our risk for heart disease.

Sleep

Bedtime	
Wake Time	
Sleep Hours	

Environmental Toxins

Internal toxins are all carcinogenic by nature, making risk to cancer high.

Meditation & Prayer

You will show me the path of life; in Your presence is fullness of joy; at Your right hand are pleasures forevermore.—Psalm 16:11

Commitment for Tomorrow:

7 Golden Keys	Commitment
Hydration	
Nutrition	
Exercise	
Sleep	
Stress	
Environmental Toxins	
Meditation & Prayer	

date: _____

7 Golden Keys	Standard	Poor	Fair	Excellent
Hydration	8–12 glasses Spring Water			
Nutrition	Four Corners Program			
Exercise	Minimum 30 minutes/day, 5–6 times/week			
Sleep	7–8.5 hours/day			
Stress	Do you feel burdened or relaxed & calm? Excellent—calm, Poor—burdened			
Environmental Toxins	Do you know the dangers & are you taking steps in your control?			
Meditation & Prayer	Excellent—daily, Poor—none			

Comments:

Commitment for Next Week:

day 15

date: _____

Hydration 8 oz. glasses of spring water

(1) (2) (3) (4) (5) (6) (7) (8) (9) (10) (11) (12)

Nutrition Foundation

time	source	description	X
am/pm		Protein	
am/pm		Healthy Fats	
am/pm		Fiber	
am/pm		Omega 3 EPA/DHA	
am/pm		Antioxidants	
am/pm		Vitamins	
am/pm		Minerals	
am/pm		Probiotics	
am/pm		Herbs	
am/pm		Enzymes	
am/pm		Amino Acids	

OR

time	product	description	X
am/pm	**LIVING FUEL Rx** Super Greens and/or Super Berry	Enzymes, Probiotic, Amino Acids, Herbs, Antioxidants, Vitamins and Minerals	
am/pm	**LIVING FUEL Rx** Omega 3 & E	Antioxidant protected fish oil caplets. Contains Omega 3 Fatty Acids with EPA & DHA	

Vegetables (Super Health Shopping List)

1	2	3	4	5	6	7	8

Fruits

1	2	3

Meals

time	description
am/pm	
am/pm	
am/pm	

Snacks

time	product	description	comments
am/pm			
am/pm			
am/pm			

Special Supplementation

time	product	time	product
am/pm		am/pm	
am/pm		am/pm	
am/pm		am/pm	

Exercise

cardio	time
Walk	
Running	
Biking	
Rowing	
Swimming	
Elliptical	
Other	

deep breathing exercises		minutes

strength	✓	time
7 Tiger Moves		
Additional Isoflexion. See Golden Key #3 Exercise.		
Other		
Stretching		

Stress

Stress management can make us less susceptible to colds and flu.

Sleep

Bedtime	
Wake Time	
Sleep Hours	

Environmental Toxins

In the 1960s only one in five people developed cancer in their lives. Now the odds are one in every two people.

Meditation & Prayer

"Call upon Me in the day of trouble; I will deliver you, and you shall glorify Me."—Psalm 50:15

Commitment for Tomorrow:

7 Golden Keys	Commitment
Hydration	
Nutrition	
Exercise	
Sleep	
Stress	
Environmental Toxins	
Meditation & Prayer	

 **day 16**

date: _____

Hydration 8 oz. glasses of spring water

(1) (2) (3) (4) (5) (6) (7) (8) (9) (10) (11) (12)

Nutrition Foundation

time	source	description	X
am/pm		Protein	
am/pm		Healthy Fats	
am/pm		Fiber	
am/pm		Omega 3 EPA/DHA	
am/pm		Antioxidants	
am/pm		Vitamins	
am/pm		Minerals	
am/pm		Probiotics	
am/pm		Herbs	
am/pm		Enzymes	
am/pm		Amino Acids	

OR

time	product	description	X
am/pm	**LIVING FUEL Rx** Super Greens and/or Super Berry	Enzymes, Probiotic, Amino Acids, Herbs, Antioxidants, Vitamins and Minerals	
am/pm	**LIVING FUEL Rx** Omega 3 & E	Antioxidant protected fish oil caplets. Contains Omega 3 Fatty Acids with EPA & DHA	

Vegetables (Super Health Shopping List)

1	2	3	4	5	6	7	8

Fruits

1	2	3

Meals

time	description
am/pm	
am/pm	
am/pm	

Snacks

time	product	description	comments
am/pm			
am/pm			
am/pm			

Special Supplementation

time	product	time	product
am/pm		am/pm	
am/pm		am/pm	
am/pm		am/pm	

Exercise

deep breathing exercises		minutes

cardio	time
Walk	
Running	
Biking	
Rowing	
Swimming	
Elliptical	
Other	

strength	✓	time
7 Tiger Moves		
Additional Isoflexion. See Golden Key #3 Exercise.		
Other		
Stretching		

Stress

The ability to handle stress positively and proactively in everyday life can alleviate the constant activation of the endocrine system.

Sleep

Bedtime	
Wake Time	
Sleep Hours	

Environmental Toxins

We all have the capacity to effect change on a personal and local level.

Meditation & Prayer

Do not be rash with your mouth, and let not your heart utter anything hastily before God. For God is in heaven, and you on earth; therefore let your words be few.—Ecclesiastes 5:2

Commitment for Tomorrow:

7 Golden Keys	Commitment
Hydration	
Nutrition	
Exercise	
Sleep	
Stress	
Environmental Toxins	
Meditation & Prayer	

 **day 17**

*date:*_____

Hydration 8 oz. glasses of spring water

 1   2   3 4 5 6 7 8 9 10 11 12

Nutrition Foundation

time	source	description	X
am/pm		Protein	
am/pm		Healthy Fats	
am/pm		Fiber	
am/pm		Omega 3 EPA/DHA	
am/pm		Antioxidants	
am/pm		Vitamins	
am/pm		Minerals	
am/pm		Probiotics	
am/pm		Herbs	
am/pm		Enzymes	
am/pm		Amino Acids	

OR

time	product	description	X
am/pm	**LIVING FUEL Rx** Super Greens and/or Super Berry	Enzymes, Probiotic, Amino Acids, Herbs, Antioxidants, Vitamins and Minerals	
am/pm	**LIVING FUEL Rx** Omega 3 & E	Antioxidant protected fish oil caplets. Contains Omega 3 Fatty Acids with EPA & DHA	

Vegetables (Super Health Shopping List)

1	2	3	4	5	6	7	8

Fruits

1	2	3

Meals

time	description
am/pm	
am/pm	
am/pm	

Snacks

time	product	description	comments
am/pm			
am/pm			
am/pm			

Special Supplementation

time	product	time	product
am/pm		am/pm	
am/pm		am/pm	
am/pm		am/pm	

Exercise

cardio	time
Walk	
Running	
Biking	
Rowing	
Swimming	
Elliptical	
Other	

deep breathing exercises	minutes

strength	✓	time
7 Tiger Moves		
Additional Isoflexion. See Golden Key #3 Exercise.		
Other		
Stretching		

Stress

Decide what you want to change. Once you acknowledge the stressor, you can more effectively deal with it.

Sleep

Bedtime	
Wake Time	
Sleep Hours	

Environmental Toxins

The first place to begin making changes is in your own home.

Meditation & Prayer

"Seek the LORD while He may be found, call upon Him while He is near."
—Isaiah 55:6

Commitment for Tomorrow:

7 Golden Keys	Commitment
Hydration	
Nutrition	
Exercise	
Sleep	
Stress	
Environmental Toxins	
Meditation & Prayer	

day 18

date: _____

Hydration 8 oz. glasses of spring water

 1   2   3   4 5   6   7 8   9   10 11   12

Nutrition Foundation

time	source	description	X
am/pm		Protein	
am/pm		Healthy Fats	
am/pm		Fiber	
am/pm		Omega 3 EPA/DHA	
am/pm		Antioxidants	
am/pm		Vitamins	
am/pm		Minerals	
am/pm		Probiotics	
am/pm		Herbs	
am/pm		Enzymes	
am/pm		Amino Acids	

OR

time	product	description	X
am/pm	**LIVING FUEL Rx** Super Greens and/or Super Berry	Enzymes, Probiotic, Amino Acids, Herbs, Antioxidants, Vitamins and Minerals	
am/pm	**LIVING FUEL Rx** Omega 3 & E	Antioxidant protected fish oil caplets. Contains Omega 3 Fatty Acids with EPA & DHA	

Vegetables (Super Health Shopping List)

1	2	3	4	5	6	7	8

Fruits

1	2	3

Meals

time	description
am/pm	
am/pm	
am/pm	

Snacks

time	product	description	comments
am/pm			
am/pm			
am/pm			

Special Supplementation

time	product	time	product
am/pm		am/pm	
am/pm		am/pm	
am/pm		am/pm	

Exercise

cardio	time
Walk	
Running	
Biking	
Rowing	
Swimming	
Elliptical	
Other	

deep breathing exercises		minutes

strength	✓	time
7 Tiger Moves		
Additional Isoflexion. See Golden Key #3 Exercise.		
Other		
Stretching		

Stress

Gauge and monitor your emotional reactions to stress. Are you overreacting? Are you reacting rather than acting?

Sleep

Bedtime	
Wake Time	
Sleep Hours	

Environmental Toxins

Plastic is everywhere and used in everything, and yet few of us understand how toxic it is.

Meditation & Prayer

"He shall pray to God, and He will delight in him, he shall see His face with joy, for He restores to man His righteousness."—Job 33:26

Commitment for Tomorrow:

7 Golden Keys	Commitment
Hydration	
Nutrition	
Exercise	
Sleep	
Stress	
Environmental Toxins	
Meditation & Prayer	

day 18

date: _____

Hydration 8oz. glasses of spring water

(1) (2) (3) (4) (5) (6) (7) (8) (9) (10) (11) (12)

Nutrition Foundation

time	source	description	X
am/pm		Protein	
am/pm		Healthy Fats	
am/pm		Fiber	
am/pm		Omega 3 EPA/DHA	
am/pm		Antioxidants	
am/pm		Vitamins	
am/pm		Minerals	
am/pm		Probiotics	
am/pm		Herbs	
am/pm		Enzymes	
am/pm		Amino Acids	

OR

time	product	description	X
am/pm	**LIVING FUEL Rx** Super Greens and/or Super Berry	Enzymes, Probiotic, Amino Acids, Herbs, Antioxidants, Vitamins and Minerals	
am/pm	**LIVING FUEL Rx** Omega 3 & E	Antioxidant protected fish oil caplets. Contains Omega 3 Fatty Acids with EPA & DHA	

Vegetables (Super Health Shopping List)

1	2	3	4	5	6	7	8

Fruits

1	2	3

Meals

time	description
am/pm	
am/pm	
am/pm	

Snacks

time	product	description	comments
am/pm			
am/pm			
am/pm			

Special Supplementation

time	product	time	product
am/pm		am/pm	
am/pm		am/pm	
am/pm		am/pm	

Exercise

cardio	time
Walk	
Running	
Biking	
Rowing	
Swimming	
Elliptical	
Other	

deep breathing exercises	minutes

strength	✓	time
7 Tiger Moves		
Additional Isoflexion. See Golden Key #3 Exercise.		
Other		
Stretching		

Stress

Breathing and relaxation techniques can take you from those agitated, white-knuckled stress responses to a place of calm and stability.

Sleep

Bedtime	
Wake Time	
Sleep Hours	

Environmental Toxins

Water that has been sitting in hot warehouses in plastic bottles is contaminated with plasticizers.

Meditation & Prayer

Evening and morning and at noon I will pray, and cry aloud, and He shall hear my voice.—Psalm 55:17

Commitment for Tomorrow:

7 Golden Keys	Commitment
Hydration	
Nutrition	
Exercise	
Sleep	
Stress	
Environmental Toxins	
Meditation & Prayer	

 **day 20**

*date:*_____

Hydration 8 oz. glasses of spring water

 1   2   3 4 5 6 7 8 9 10 11 12

Nutrition Foundation

time	source	description	X
am/pm		Protein	
am/pm		Healthy Fats	
am/pm		Fiber	
am/pm		Omega 3 EPA/DHA	
am/pm		Antioxidants	
am/pm		Vitamins	
am/pm		Minerals	
am/pm		Probiotics	
am/pm		Herbs	
am/pm		Enzymes	
am/pm		Amino Acids	

OR

time	product	description	X
am/pm	**LIVING FUEL Rx** Super Greens and/or Super Berry	Enzymes, Probiotic, Amino Acids, Herbs, Antioxidants, Vitamins and Minerals	
am/pm	**LIVING FUEL Rx** Omega 3 & E	Antioxidant protected fish oil caplets. Contains Omega 3 Fatty Acids with EPA & DHA	

Vegetables (Super Health Shopping List)

1	2	3	4	5	6	7	8

Fruits

1	2	3

Meals

time	description
am/pm	
am/pm	
am/pm	

Snacks

time	product	description	comments
am/pm			
am/pm			
am/pm			

Special Supplementation

time	product	time	product
am/pm		am/pm	
am/pm		am/pm	
am/pm		am/pm	

Exercise

cardio	time
Walk	
Running	
Biking	
Rowing	
Swimming	
Elliptical	
Other	

deep breathing exercises	minutes

strength	✓	time
7 Tiger Moves		
Additional Isoflexion. See Golden Key #3 Exercise.		
Other		
Stretching		

Stress

Eating healthy, exercising regularly, and getting enough sleep will give you the physical stamina you need when stress begins.

Sleep

Bedtime	
Wake Time	
Sleep Hours	

Environmental Toxins

PET or PETE is generally considered the safest *single-use* plastic bottle choice.

Meditation & Prayer

So He said to them, "When you pray, say: Our Father in heaven, hallowed be Your name. Your kingdom come. Your will be done on earth as it is in heaven."—Luke 11:2

Commitment for Tomorrow:

7 Golden Keys	Commitment
Hydration	
Nutrition	
Exercise	
Sleep	
Stress	
Environmental Toxins	
Meditation & Prayer	

day 21

date: _____

Hydration   8 oz. glasses of spring water

(1) (2) (3) (4) (5) (6) (7) (8) (9) (10) (11) (12)

Nutrition Foundation

time	source	description	X
am/pm		Protein	
am/pm		Healthy Fats	
am/pm		Fiber	
am/pm		Omega 3 EPA/DHA	
am/pm		Antioxidants	
am/pm		Vitamins	
am/pm		Minerals	
am/pm		Probiotics	
am/pm		Herbs	
am/pm		Enzymes	
am/pm		Amino Acids	

OR

time	product	description	X
am/pm	**LIVING FUEL Rx** Super Greens and/or Super Berry	Enzymes, Probiotic, Amino Acids, Herbs, Antioxidants, Vitamins and Minerals	
am/pm	**LIVING FUEL Rx** Omega 3 & E	Antioxidant protected fish oil caplets. Contains Omega 3 Fatty Acids with EPA & DHA	

Vegetables (Super Health Shopping List)

1	2	3	4	5	6	7	8

Fruits

1	2	3

Meals

time	description
am/pm	
am/pm	
am/pm	

Snacks

time	product	description	comments
am/pm			
am/pm			
am/pm			

Special Supplementation

time	product	time	product
am/pm		am/pm	
am/pm		am/pm	
am/pm		am/pm	

Exercise

cardio	time
Walk	
Running	
Biking	
Rowing	
Swimming	
Elliptical	
Other	

deep breathing exercises	minutes

strength	✓	time
7 Tiger Moves		
Additional Isoflexion. See Golden Key #3 Exercise.		
Other		
Stretching		

Stress

Each week, make sure you give yourself a day of rest and relaxation.

Sleep

Bedtime	
Wake Time	
Sleep Hours	

Environmental Toxins

Use PETE or PET plastics—they are brighter than PVC plastic, very transparent, and almost look like glass.

Meditation & Prayer

"But from there you will seek the LORD your God, and you will find Him if you seek Him with all your heart and with all your soul."—Deuteronomy 4:29

Commitment for Tomorrow:

7 Golden Keys	Commitment
Hydration	
Nutrition	
Exercise	
Sleep	
Stress	
Environmental Toxins	
Meditation & Prayer	

date: _____

7 Golden Keys	Standard	Poor	Fair	Excellent
Hydration	8–12 glasses Spring Water			
Nutrition	Four Corners Program			
Exercise	Minimum 30 minutes/day, 5–6 times/week			
Sleep	7–8.5 hours/day			
Stress	Do you feel burdened or relaxed & calm? Excellent—calm, Poor—burdened			
Environmental Toxins	Do you know the dangers & are you taking steps in your control?			
Meditation & Prayer	Excellent—daily, Poor—none			

Comments:

Commitment for Next Week:

week 3

day 22

Hydration 8 oz. glasses of spring water

(1) (2) (3) (4) (5) (6) (7) (8) (9) (10) (11) (12)

Nutrition Foundation

time	source	description	X
am/pm		Protein	
am/pm		Healthy Fats	
am/pm		Fiber	
am/pm		Omega 3 EPA/DHA	
am/pm		Antioxidants	
am/pm		Vitamins	
am/pm		Minerals	
am/pm		Probiotics	
am/pm		Herbs	
am/pm		Enzymes	
am/pm		Amino Acids	

OR

time	product	description	X
am/pm	**LIVING FUEL Rx** Super Greens and/or Super Berry	Enzymes, Probiotic, Amino Acids, Herbs, Antioxidants, Vitamins and Minerals	
am/pm	**LIVING FUEL Rx** Omega 3 & E	Antioxidant protected fish oil caplets. Contains Omega 3 Fatty Acids with EPA & DHA	

Vegetables (Super Health Shopping List)

1	2	3	4	5	6	7	8

Fruits

1	2	3

Meals

time	description
am/pm	
am/pm	
am/pm	

Snacks

time	product	description	comments
am/pm			
am/pm			
am/pm			

Special Supplementation

time	product	time	product
am/pm		am/pm	
am/pm		am/pm	
am/pm		am/pm	

Exercise

cardio	time
Walk	
Running	
Biking	
Rowing	
Swimming	
Elliptical	
Other	

deep breathing exercises		minutes

strength	✓	time
7 Tiger Moves		
Additional Isoflexion. See Golden Key #3 Exercise.		
Other		
Stretching		

Stress

Exercise makes us more robust and better equipped to fight stress and disease.

Sleep

Bedtime	
Wake Time	
Sleep Hours	

Environmental Toxins

Minimize drinking out of or storing food in plastics of any kind.

Meditation & Prayer

O God, You are my God; early will I seek You; my soul thirsts for You; my flesh longs for You in a dry and thirsty land where there is no water.
—Psalm 63:1

Commitment for Tomorrow:

7 Golden Keys	Commitment
Hydration	
Nutrition	
Exercise	
Sleep	
Stress	
Environmental Toxins	
Meditation & Prayer	

 **day 23**

*date:*_____

Hydration 8 oz. glasses of spring water

 1 2 3 4 5 6 7 8 9 10 11 12

Nutrition Foundation

time	source	description	X
am/pm		Protein	
am/pm		Healthy Fats	
am/pm		Fiber	
am/pm		Omega 3 EPA/DHA	
am/pm		Antioxidants	
am/pm		Vitamins	
am/pm		Minerals	
am/pm		Probiotics	
am/pm		Herbs	
am/pm		Enzymes	
am/pm		Amino Acids	

OR

time	product	description	X
am/pm	**LIVING FUEL Rx** Super Greens and/or Super Berry	Enzymes, Probiotic, Amino Acids, Herbs, Antioxidants, Vitamins and Minerals	
am/pm	**LIVING FUEL Rx** Omega 3 & E	Antioxidant protected fish oil caplets. Contains Omega 3 Fatty Acids with EPA & DHA	

Vegetables (Super Health Shopping LIst)

1	2	3	4	5	6	7	8

Fruits

1	2	3

Meals

time	description
am/pm	
am/pm	
am/pm	

Snacks

time	product	description	comments
am/pm			
am/pm			
am/pm			

Special Supplementation

time	product	time	product
am/pm		am/pm	
am/pm		am/pm	
am/pm		am/pm	

Exercise

cardio	time
Walk	
Running	
Biking	
Rowing	
Swimming	
Elliptical	
Other	

deep breathing exercises	minutes

strength	✓	time
7 Tiger Moves		
Additional Isoflexion. See Golden Key #3 Exercise.		
Other		
Stretching		

Stress

Competition and high-risk activities are examples of good stress.

Sleep

Bedtime	
Wake Time	
Sleep Hours	

Environmental Toxins

Buy your water in glass water bottles.

Meditation & Prayer

"Call to Me, and I will answer you, and show you great and mighty things, which you do not know."—Jeremiah 33:3

Commitment for Tomorrow:

7 Golden Keys	Commitment
Hydration	
Nutrition	
Exercise	
Sleep	
Stress	
Environmental Toxins	
Meditation & Prayer	

 **day 24**

date: _____

Hydration 8 oz. glasses of spring water

 1 2 3 4 5 6 7 8 9 10 11 12

Nutrition Foundation

time	source	description	X
am/pm		Protein	
am/pm		Healthy Fats	
am/pm		Fiber	
am/pm		Omega 3 EPA/DHA	
am/pm		Antioxidants	
am/pm		Vitamins	
am/pm		Minerals	
am/pm		Probiotics	
am/pm		Herbs	
am/pm		Enzymes	
am/pm		Amino Acids	

OR

time	product	description	X
am/pm	**LIVING FUEL Rx** Super Greens and/or Super Berry	Enzymes, Probiotic, Amino Acids, Herbs, Antioxidants, Vitamins and Minerals	
am/pm	**LIVING FUEL Rx** Omega 3 & E	Antioxidant protected fish oil caplets. Contains Omega 3 Fatty Acids with EPA & DHA	

Vegetables (Super Health Shopping List)

1	2	3	4	5	6	7	8

Fruits

1	2	3

Meals

time	description
am/pm	
am/pm	
am/pm	

Snacks

time	product	description	comments
am/pm			
am/pm			
am/pm			

Special Supplementation

time	product	time	product
am/pm		am/pm	
am/pm		am/pm	
am/pm		am/pm	

Exercise

cardio	time
Walk	
Running	
Biking	
Rowing	
Swimming	
Elliptical	
Other	

deep breathing exercises	minutes

strength	✓	time
7 Tiger Moves		
Additional Isoflexion. See Golden Key #3 Exercise.		
Other		
Stretching		

Stress

Learn how to prioritize; this means deciding what is truly critical and what is not.

Sleep

Bedtime	
Wake Time	
Sleep Hours	

Environmental Toxins

Choose a pacifier made of silicon rather than plastic for your baby.

Meditation & Prayer

"If you then, being evil, know how to give good gifts to your children, how much more will your Father who is in heaven give good things to those who ask Him!"—Matthew 7:11

Commitment for Tomorrow:

7 Golden Keys	Commitment
Hydration	
Nutrition	
Exercise	
Sleep	
Stress	
Environmental Toxins	
Meditation & Prayer	

day 25

date: _____

Hydration   8 oz. glasses of spring water

① ② ③ ④ ⑤ ⑥ ⑦ ⑧ ⑨ ⑩ ⑪ ⑫

Nutrition Foundation

time	source	description	X
am/pm		Protein	
am/pm		Healthy Fats	
am/pm		Fiber	
am/pm		Omega 3 EPA/DHA	
am/pm		Antioxidants	
am/pm		Vitamins	
am/pm		Minerals	
am/pm		Probiotics	
am/pm		Herbs	
am/pm		Enzymes	
am/pm		Amino Acids	

OR

time	product	description	X
am/pm	**LIVING FUEL Rx** Super Greens and/or Super Berry	Enzymes, Probiotic, Amino Acids, Herbs, Antioxidants, Vitamins and Minerals	
am/pm	**LIVING FUEL Rx** Omega 3 & E	Antioxidant protected fish oil caplets. Contains Omega 3 Fatty Acids with EPA & DHA	

Vegetables (Super Health Shopping List)

1	2	3	4	5	6	7	8

Fruits

1	2	3

Meals

time	description
am/pm	
am/pm	
am/pm	

Snacks

time	product	description	comments
am/pm			
am/pm			
am/pm			

Special Supplementation

time	product	time	product
am/pm		am/pm	
am/pm		am/pm	
am/pm		am/pm	

Exercise

cardio	time
Walk	
Running	
Biking	
Rowing	
Swimming	
Elliptical	
Other	

deep breathing exercises		minutes

strength	✓	time
7 Tiger Moves		
Additional Isoflexion. See Golden Key #3 Exercise.		
Other		
Stretching		

Stress

One of the reasons chronic stress is a killer is because of all the excess free radicals that are produced and released.

Sleep

Bedtime	
Wake Time	
Sleep Hours	

Environmental Toxins

An essential key to health and to reverse aging is identifying and eliminating the toxins from our life.

Meditation & Prayer

Now to Him who is able to do exceedingly abundantly above all that we ask or think, according to the power that works in us.—Ephesians 3:20

Commitment for Tomorrow:

7 Golden Keys	Commitment
Hydration	
Nutrition	
Exercise	
Sleep	
Stress	
Environmental Toxins	
Meditation & Prayer	

day 26

date: _____

Hydration 8 oz. glasses of spring water

(1) (2) (3) (4) (5) (6) (7) (8) (9) (10) (11) (12)

Nutrition Foundation

time	source	description	X
am/pm		Protein	
am/pm		Healthy Fats	
am/pm		Fiber	
am/pm		Omega 3 EPA/DHA	
am/pm		Antioxidants	
am/pm		Vitamins	
am/pm		Minerals	
am/pm		Probiotics	
am/pm		Herbs	
am/pm		Enzymes	
am/pm		Amino Acids	

OR

time	product	description	X
am/pm	**LIVING FUEL Rx** Super Greens and/or Super Berry	Enzymes, Probiotic, Amino Acids, Herbs, Antioxidants, Vitamins and Minerals	
am/pm	**LIVING FUEL Rx** Omega 3 & E	Antioxidant protected fish oil caplets. Contains Omega 3 Fatty Acids with EPA & DHA	

Vegetables (Super Health Shopping List)

1	2	3	4	5	6	7	8

Fruits

1	2	3

Meals

time	description
am/pm	
am/pm	
am/pm	

Snacks

time	product	description	comments
am/pm			
am/pm			
am/pm			

Special Supplementation

time	product	time	product
am/pm		am/pm	
am/pm		am/pm	
am/pm		am/pm	

Exercise

cardio	time
Walk	
Running	
Biking	
Rowing	
Swimming	
Elliptical	
Other	

deep breathing exercises		minutes
strength	✓	time
7 Tiger Moves		
Additional Isoflexion. See Golden Key #3 Exercise.		
Other		
Stretching		

Stress

Antioxidants and omega-3 fish oils can prevent your cell membranes from oxidating and becoming rancid.

Sleep

Bedtime	
Wake Time	
Sleep Hours	

Environmental Toxins

The food processing industry adds more than 3,000 chemicals to our food annually.

Meditation & Prayer

"Consecrate yourselves therefore, and be holy, for I am the LORD your God. And you shall keep My statutes, and perform them: I am the LORD who sanctifies you."—Leviticus 20:7–8

Commitment for Tomorrow:

7 Golden Keys	Commitment
Hydration	
Nutrition	
Exercise	
Sleep	
Stress	
Environmental Toxins	
Meditation & Prayer	

day 29

 **day 27**

date: _____

Hydration   8 oz. glasses of spring water

(1) (2) (3) (4) (5) (6) (7) (8) (9) (10) (11) (12)

Nutrition Foundation

time	source	description	X
am/pm		Protein	
am/pm		Healthy Fats	
am/pm		Fiber	
am/pm		Omega 3 EPA/DHA	
am/pm		Antioxidants	
am/pm		Vitamins	
am/pm		Minerals	
am/pm		Probiotics	
am/pm		Herbs	
am/pm		Enzymes	
am/pm		Amino Acids	

OR

time	product	description	X
am/pm	**LIVING FUEL Rx** Super Greens and/or Super Berry	Enzymes, Probiotic, Amino Acids, Herbs, Antioxidants, Vitamins and Minerals	
am/pm	**LIVING FUEL Rx** Omega 3 & E	Antioxidant protected fish oil caplets. Contains Omega 3 Fatty Acids with EPA & DHA	

Vegetables (Super Health Shopping List)

1	2	3	4	5	6	7	8

Fruits

1	2	3

Meals

time	description
am/pm	
am/pm	
am/pm	

Snacks

time	product	description	comments
am/pm			
am/pm			
am/pm			

Special Supplementation

time	product	time	product
am/pm		am/pm	
am/pm		am/pm	
am/pm		am/pm	

Exercise

cardio	time
Walk	
Running	
Biking	
Rowing	
Swimming	
Elliptical	
Other	

deep breathing exercises		minutes
strength	✓	time
7 Tiger Moves		
Additional Isoflexion. See Golden Key #3 Exercise.		
Other		
Stretching		

Stress

A high dietary intake of Vitamin C may help reduce the effects of chronic stress.

Sleep

Bedtime	
Wake Time	
Sleep Hours	

Environmental Toxins

About 60 percent of herbicides, 90 percent of fungicides, and 30 percent of insecticides are known to be carcinogenic.

Meditation & Prayer

"For the LORD your God is He who goes with you, to fight for you against your enemies, to save you."—Deuteronomy 20:4

Commitment for Tomorrow:

7 Golden Keys	Commitment
Hydration	
Nutrition	
Exercise	
Sleep	
Stress	
Environmental Toxins	
Meditation & Prayer	

date: _____

Hydration 8 oz. glasses of spring water

(1) (2) (3) (4) (5) (6) (7) (8) (9) (10) (11) (12)

Nutrition Foundation

time	source	description	X
am/pm		Protein	
am/pm		Healthy Fats	
am/pm		Fiber	
am/pm		Omega 3 EPA/DHA	
am/pm		Antioxidants	
am/pm		Vitamins	
am/pm		Minerals	
am/pm		Probiotics	
am/pm		Herbs	
am/pm		Enzymes	
am/pm		Amino Acids	

OR

time	product	description	X
am/pm	**LIVING FUEL Rx** Super Greens and/or Super Berry	Enzymes, Probiotic, Amino Acids, Herbs, Antioxidants, Vitamins and Minerals	
am/pm	**LIVING FUEL Rx** Omega 3 & E	Antioxidant protected fish oil caplets. Contains Omega 3 Fatty Acids with EPA & DHA	

Vegetables (Super Health Shopping List)

1	2	3	4	5	6	7	8

Fruits

1	2	3

Meals

time	description
am/pm	
am/pm	
am/pm	

Snacks

time	product	description	comments
am/pm			
am/pm			
am/pm			

Special Supplementation

time	product	time	product
am/pm		am/pm	
am/pm		am/pm	
am/pm		am/pm	

Exercise

cardio	time
Walk	
Running	
Biking	
Rowing	
Swimming	
Elliptical	
Other	

deep breathing exercises		minutes

strength	✓	time
7 Tiger Moves		
Additional Isoflexion. See Golden Key #3 Exercise.		
Other		
Stretching		

Stress

Avoid caffeine and high glycemic foods, such as soft drinks and candy.

Sleep

Bedtime	
Wake Time	
Sleep Hours	

Environmental Toxins

The FDA reported that human cells appear to be very sensitive to gamma radiation and the altered byproducts in irradiated food.

Meditation & Prayer

"As for me and my house, we will serve the LORD."—Joshua 24:15

Commitment for Tomorrow:

7 Golden Keys	Commitment
Hydration	
Nutrition	
Exercise	
Sleep	
Stress	
Environmental Toxins	
Meditation & Prayer	

day 28

week 4 summary

date: _____

7 Golden Keys	Standard	Poor	Fair	Excellent
Hydration	8–12 glasses Spring Water			
Nutrition	Four Corners Program			
Exercise	Minimum 30 minutes/day, 5–6 times/week			
Sleep	7–8.5 hours/day			
Stress	Do you feel burdened or relaxed & calm? Excellent—calm, Poor—burdened			
Environmental Toxins	Do you know the dangers & are you taking steps in your control?			
Meditation & Prayer	Excellent—daily, Poor—none			

Comments:

Commitment for Next Week:

Week 4

day 29

date: _____

Hydration 8 oz. glasses of spring water

(1)　(2)　(3)　(4)　(5)　(6)　(7)　(8)　(9)　(10)　(11)　(12)

Nutrition Foundation

time	source	description	X
am/pm		Protein	
am/pm		Healthy Fats	
am/pm		Fiber	
am/pm		Omega 3 EPA/DHA	
am/pm		Antioxidants	
am/pm		Vitamins	
am/pm		Minerals	
am/pm		Probiotics	
am/pm		Herbs	
am/pm		Enzymes	
am/pm		Amino Acids	

OR

time	product	description	X
am/pm	**LIVING FUEL Rx** Super Greens and/or Super Berry	Enzymes, Probiotic, Amino Acids, Herbs, Antioxidants, Vitamins and Minerals	
am/pm	**LIVING FUEL Rx** Omega 3 & E	Antioxidant protected fish oil caplets. Contains Omega 3 Fatty Acids with EPA & DHA	

Vegetables (Super Health Shopping List)

1	2	3	4	5	6	7	8

Fruits

1	2	3

Meals

time	description
am/pm	
am/pm	
am/pm	

Snacks

time	product	description	comments
am/pm			
am/pm			
am/pm			

Special Supplementation

time	product	time	product
am/pm		am/pm	
am/pm		am/pm	
am/pm		am/pm	

Exercise

cardio	time
Walk	
Running	
Biking	
Rowing	
Swimming	
Elliptical	
Other	

deep breathing exercises	minutes

strength	✓	time
7 Tiger Moves		
Additional Isoflexion. See Golden Key #3 Exercise.		
Other		
Stretching		

Stress

Why not go for a long walk, read a good book, or spend the afternoon playing with the children?

Sleep

Bedtime	
Wake Time	
Sleep Hours	

Environmental Toxins

The one mineral that has been conclusively demonstrated to protect us from toxicity-induced cancers is the trace mineral selenium.

Meditation & Prayer

"The Spirit of God has made me, and the breath of the Almighty gives me life."—Job 33:4

Commitment for Tomorrow:

7 Golden Keys	Commitment
Hydration	
Nutrition	
Exercise	
Sleep	
Stress	
Environmental Toxins	
Meditation & Prayer	

day 30

date: _____

Hydration 8oz. glasses of spring water

(1) (2) (3) (4) (5) (6) (7) (8) (9) (10) (11) (12)

Nutrition Foundation

time	source	description	X
am/pm		Protein	
am/pm		Healthy Fats	
am/pm		Fiber	
am/pm		Omega 3 EPA/DHA	
am/pm		Antioxidants	
am/pm		Vitamins	
am/pm		Minerals	
am/pm		Probiotics	
am/pm		Herbs	
am/pm		Enzymes	
am/pm		Amino Acids	

OR

time	product	description	X
am/pm	**LIVING FUEL Rx** Super Greens and/or Super Berry	Enzymes, Probiotic, Amino Acids, Herbs, Antioxidants, Vitamins and Minerals	
am/pm	**LIVING FUEL Rx** Omega 3 & E	Antioxidant protected fish oil caplets. Contains Omega 3 Fatty Acids with EPA & DHA	

Vegetables (Super Health Shopping List)

1	2	3	4	5	6	7	8

Fruits

1	2	3

Meals

time	description
am/pm	
am/pm	
am/pm	

Snacks

time	product	description	comments
am/pm			
am/pm			
am/pm			

Special Supplementation

time	product	time	product
am/pm		am/pm	
am/pm		am/pm	
am/pm		am/pm	

Exercise

cardio	time
Walk	
Running	
Biking	
Rowing	
Swimming	
Elliptical	
Other	

deep breathing exercises	minutes

strength	✓	time
7 Tiger Moves		
Additional Isoflexion. See Golden Key #3 Exercise.		
Other		
Stretching		

Stress

Plant some flowers, draw a picture, or enjoy a leisurely meal (organic, of course) with some friends.

Sleep

Bedtime	
Wake Time	
Sleep Hours	

Environmental Toxins

GMO seeds and crops do not have good nutrition levels.

Meditation & Prayer

"Heal me, O LORD, and I shall be healed; save me, and I shall be saved, for you are my praise."—Jeremiah 17:14

Commitment for Tomorrow:

7 Golden Keys	Commitment
Hydration	
Nutrition	
Exercise	
Sleep	
Stress	
Environmental Toxins	
Meditation & Prayer	

 **day 31**   *date:* _____

Hydration   8 oz. glasses of spring water

 1   2   3   4   5   6   7   8   9   10   11   12

Nutrition Foundation

time	source	description	X
am/pm		Protein	
am/pm		Healthy Fats	
am/pm		Fiber	
am/pm		Omega 3 EPA/DHA	
am/pm		Antioxidants	
am/pm		Vitamins	
am/pm		Minerals	
am/pm		Probiotics	
am/pm		Herbs	
am/pm		Enzymes	
am/pm		Amino Acids	

OR

time	product	description	X
am/pm	**LIVING FUEL Rx** Super Greens and/or Super Berry	Enzymes, Probiotic, Amino Acids, Herbs, Antioxidants, Vitamins and Minerals	
am/pm	**LIVING FUEL Rx** Omega 3 & E	Antioxidant protected fish oil caplets. Contains Omega 3 Fatty Acids with EPA & DHA	

Vegetables (Super Health Shopping List)

1	2	3	4	5	6	7	8

Fruits

1	2	3

Meals

time	description
am/pm	
am/pm	
am/pm	

Snacks

time	product	description	comments
am/pm			
am/pm			
am/pm			

Special Supplementation

time	product	time	product
am/pm		am/pm	
am/pm		am/pm	
am/pm		am/pm	

Exercise

deep breathing exercises	minutes

cardio	time
Walk	
Running	
Biking	
Rowing	
Swimming	
Elliptical	
Other	

strength	✓	time
7 Tiger Moves		
Additional Isoflexion. See Golden Key #3 Exercise.		
Other		
Stretching		

Stress

"The bow always strung…will not do."—George Eliot

Sleep

Bedtime	
Wake Time	
Sleep Hours	

Environmental Toxins

Eat only whole, natural organic foods.

Meditation & Prayer

"Ah, LORD GOD! Behold, You have made the heavens and the earth by Your great power and outstretched arm. There is nothing too hard for You."
—Jeremiah 32:17

Commitment for Tomorrow:

7 Golden Keys	Commitment
Hydration	
Nutrition	
Exercise	
Sleep	
Stress	
Environmental Toxins	
Meditation & Prayer	

day 31

day 32

date: _____

Hydration   8 oz. glasses of spring water

 1   2   3   4   5   6   7   8   9   10   11   12

Nutrition Foundation

time	source	description	X
am/pm		Protein	
am/pm		Healthy Fats	
am/pm		Fiber	
am/pm		Omega 3 EPA/DHA	
am/pm		Antioxidants	
am/pm		Vitamins	
am/pm		Minerals	
am/pm		Probiotics	
am/pm		Herbs	
am/pm		Enzymes	
am/pm		Amino Acids	

OR

time	product	description	X
am/pm	**LIVING FUEL Rx** Super Greens and/or Super Berry	Enzymes, Probiotic, Amino Acids, Herbs, Antioxidants, Vitamins and Minerals	
am/pm	**LIVING FUEL Rx** Omega 3 & E	Antioxidant protected fish oil caplets. Contains Omega 3 Fatty Acids with EPA & DHA	

Vegetables (Super Health Shopping LIst)

1	2	3	4	5	6	7	8

Fruits

1	2	3

Meals

time	description
am/pm	
am/pm	
am/pm	

Snacks

time	product	description	comments
am/pm			
am/pm			
am/pm			

Special Supplementation

time	product	time	product
am/pm		am/pm	
am/pm		am/pm	
am/pm		am/pm	

Exercise

	cardio	time
Walk		
Running		
Biking		
Rowing		
Swimming		
Elliptical		
Other		

deep breathing exercises		minutes

strength	✓	time
7 Tiger Moves		
Additional Isoflexion. See Golden Key #3 Exercise.		
Other		
Stretching		

Stress

Rely on your faith and spiritual beliefs during times of anxiety and distress.

Sleep

Bedtime	
Wake Time	
Sleep Hours	

Environmental Toxins

Avoid all fortified or enriched foods.

Meditation & Prayer

In God I have put my trust; I will not be afraid. What can man do to me?
—Psalm 56:11

Commitment for Tomorrow:

7 Golden Keys	Commitment
Hydration	
Nutrition	
Exercise	
Sleep	
Stress	
Environmental Toxins	
Meditation & Prayer	

 **day 33**

date: _____

Hydration 8 oz. glasses of spring water

 1   2   3   4   5   6   7   8   9   10   11 12

Nutrition Foundation

time	source	description	X
am/pm		Protein	
am/pm		Healthy Fats	
am/pm		Fiber	
am/pm		Omega 3 EPA/DHA	
am/pm		Antioxidants	
am/pm		Vitamins	
am/pm		Minerals	
am/pm		Probiotics	
am/pm		Herbs	
am/pm		Enzymes	
am/pm		Amino Acids	

OR

time	product	description	X
am/pm	**LIVING FUEL Rx** Super Greens and/or Super Berry	Enzymes, Probiotic, Amino Acids, Herbs, Antioxidants, Vitamins and Minerals	
am/pm	**LIVING FUEL Rx** Omega 3 & E	Antioxidant protected fish oil caplets. Contains Omega 3 Fatty Acids with EPA & DHA	

Vegetables (Super Health Shopping List)

1	2	3	4	5	6	7	8

Fruits

1	2	3

Meals

time	description
am/pm	
am/pm	
am/pm	

Snacks

time	product	description	comments
am/pm			
am/pm			
am/pm			

Special Supplementation

time	product	time	product
am/pm		am/pm	
am/pm		am/pm	
am/pm		am/pm	

Exercise

cardio	time
Walk	
Running	
Biking	
Rowing	
Swimming	
Elliptical	
Other	

deep breathing exercises	minutes

strength	✓	time
7 Tiger Moves		
Additional Isoflexion. See Golden Key #3 Exercise.		
Other		
Stretching		

Stress

Relaxation and quiet reflection go very far in mitigating the stresses of modern life.

Sleep

Bedtime	
Wake Time	
Sleep Hours	

Environmental Toxins

Avoid all processed foods.

Meditation & Prayer

I will both lie down in peace, and sleep; for You alone, O LORD, make me dwell in safety.—Psalm 4:8

Commitment for Tomorrow:

7 Golden Keys	Commitment
Hydration	
Nutrition	
Exercise	
Sleep	
Stress	
Environmental Toxins	
Meditation & Prayer	

day33

 **day 34**

date: _____

Hydration 8 oz. glasses of spring water

(1) (2) (3) (4) (5) (6) (7) (8) (9) (10) (11) (12)

Nutrition Foundation

time	source	description	X
am/pm		Protein	
am/pm		Healthy Fats	
am/pm		Fiber	
am/pm		Omega 3 EPA/DHA	
am/pm		Antioxidants	
am/pm		Vitamins	
am/pm		Minerals	
am/pm		Probiotics	
am/pm		Herbs	
am/pm		Enzymes	
am/pm		Amino Acids	

OR

time	product	description	X
am/pm	**LIVING FUEL Rx** Super Greens and/or Super Berry	Enzymes, Probiotic, Amino Acids, Herbs, Antioxidants, Vitamins and Minerals	
am/pm	**LIVING FUEL Rx** Omega 3 & E	Antioxidant protected fish oil caplets. Contains Omega 3 Fatty Acids with EPA & DHA	

Vegetables (Super Health Shopping List)

1	2	3	4	5	6	7	8

Fruits

1	2	3

Meals

time	description
am/pm	
am/pm	
am/pm	

Snacks

time	product	description	comments
am/pm			
am/pm			
am/pm			

Special Supplementation

time	product	time	product
am/pm		am/pm	
am/pm		am/pm	
am/pm		am/pm	

Exercise

cardio	time
Walk	
Running	
Biking	
Rowing	
Swimming	
Elliptical	
Other	

deep breathing exercises	minutes

strength	✓	time
7 Tiger Moves		
Additional Isoflexion. See Golden Key #3 Exercise.		
Other		
Stretching		

Stress

God is our refuge and strength, a very present help in trouble.—Psalm 46:1

Sleep

Bedtime	
Wake Time	
Sleep Hours	

Environmental Toxins

Avoid eating food from airports and train stations, as the food in these locations has been irradiated.

Meditation & Prayer

This is the day the LORD has made; we will rejoice and be glad in it.
—Psalm 118:24

Commitment for Tomorrow:

7 Golden Keys	Commitment
Hydration	
Nutrition	
Exercise	
Sleep	
Stress	
Environmental Toxins	
Meditation & Prayer	

 **day 35**

date: _____

Hydration 8 oz. glasses of spring water

 1   2   3   4   5   6   7   8   9 10 11 12

Nutrition Foundation

time	source	description	X
am/pm		Protein	
am/pm		Healthy Fats	
am/pm		Fiber	
am/pm		Omega 3 EPA/DHA	
am/pm		Antioxidants	
am/pm		Vitamins	
am/pm		Minerals	
am/pm		Probiotics	
am/pm		Herbs	
am/pm		Enzymes	
am/pm		Amino Acids	

OR

time	product	description	X
am/pm	**LIVING FUEL Rx** Super Greens and/or Super Berry	Enzymes, Probiotic, Amino Acids, Herbs, Antioxidants, Vitamins and Minerals	
am/pm	**LIVING FUEL Rx** Omega 3 & E	Antioxidant protected fish oil caplets. Contains Omega 3 Fatty Acids with EPA & DHA	

Vegetables (Super Health Shopping List)

1	2	3	4	5	6	7	8

Fruits

1	2	3

Meals

time	description
am/pm	
am/pm	
am/pm	

Snacks

time	product	description	comments
am/pm			
am/pm			
am/pm			

Special Supplementation

time	product	time	product
am/pm		am/pm	
am/pm		am/pm	
am/pm		am/pm	

Exercise

cardio	time
Walk	
Running	
Biking	
Rowing	
Swimming	
Elliptical	
Other	

deep breathing exercises	minutes

strength	✓	time
7 Tiger Moves		
Additional Isoflexion. See Golden Key #3 Exercise.		
Other		
Stretching		

Stress

And let us not grow weary while doing good, for in due season we shall reap if we do not lose heart.—Galatians 6:9

Sleep

Bedtime	
Wake Time	
Sleep Hours	

Environmental Toxins

Up to 400 different toxic chemicals are used in a single perfume manufactured today.

Meditation & Prayer

Trust in the LORD with all your heart, and lean not on your own understanding; in all your ways acknowledge Him, and He shall direct your paths.—Proverbs 3:5–6

Commitment for Tomorrow:

7 Golden Keys	Commitment
Hydration	
Nutrition	
Exercise	
Sleep	
Stress	
Environmental Toxins	
Meditation & Prayer	

day 35

week 5 summary

date: _____

7 Golden Keys	Standard	Poor	Fair	Excellent
Hydration	8–12 glasses Spring Water			
Nutrition	Four Corners Program			
Exercise	Minimum 30 minutes/day, 5–6 times/week			
Sleep	7–8.5 hours/day			
Stress	Do you feel burdened or relaxed & calm? Excellent—calm, Poor—burdened			
Environmental Toxins	Do you know the dangers & are you taking steps in your control?			
Meditation & Prayer	Excellent—daily, Poor—none			

NOTE: Time to order your next *Living the Seven Keys to Lifelong Vitality Journal!*

Comments:

Commitment for Next Week:

 **day 36**

*date:*_____

Hydration 8 oz. glasses of spring water

 (1) (2) (3) (4) (5) (6) (7) (8) (9) (10) (11) (12)

Nutrition Foundation

time	source	description	X
am/pm		Protein	
am/pm		Healthy Fats	
am/pm		Fiber	
am/pm		Omega 3 EPA/DHA	
am/pm		Antioxidants	
am/pm		Vitamins	
am/pm		Minerals	
am/pm		Probiotics	
am/pm		Herbs	
am/pm		Enzymes	
am/pm		Amino Acids	

OR

time	product	description	X
am/pm	**LIVING FUEL Rx** Super Greens and/or Super Berry	Enzymes, Probiotic, Amino Acids, Herbs, Antioxidants, Vitamins and Minerals	
am/pm	**LIVING FUEL Rx** Omega 3 & E	Antioxidant protected fish oil caplets. Contains Omega 3 Fatty Acids with EPA & DHA	

Vegetables (Super Health Shopping List)

1	2	3	4	5	6	7	8

Fruits

1	2	3

Meals

time	description
am/pm	
am/pm	
am/pm	

Snacks

time	product	description	comments
am/pm			
am/pm			
am/pm			

Special Supplementation

time	product	time	product
am/pm		am/pm	
am/pm		am/pm	
am/pm		am/pm	

Exercise

cardio	time
Walk	
Running	
Biking	
Rowing	
Swimming	
Elliptical	
Other	

deep breathing exercises	minutes

strength	✓	time
7 Tiger Moves		
Additional Isoflexion. See Golden Key #3 Exercise.		
Other		
Stretching		

Stress

"For I have satiated the weary soul, and I have replenished every sorrowful soul."—Jeremiah 31:25

Sleep

Bedtime	
Wake Time	
Sleep Hours	

Environmental Toxins

The fragrance industry is a self-regulated industry, and 84 percent of these chemical ingredients have never been tested.

Meditation & Prayer

In my distress I called upon the LORD, and cried out to my God; He heard my voice from His temple, and my cry came before Him, even to His ears. —Psalm 18:6

Commitment for Tomorrow:

7 Golden Keys	Commitment
Hydration	
Nutrition	
Exercise	
Sleep	
Stress	
Environmental Toxins	
Meditation & Prayer	

 **day 37**

date: _____

Hydration 8 oz. glasses of spring water

 1   2 3   4 5   6   7   8 9   10   11 12

Nutrition Foundation

time	source	description	X
am/pm		Protein	
am/pm		Healthy Fats	
am/pm		Fiber	
am/pm		Omega 3 EPA/DHA	
am/pm		Antioxidants	
am/pm		Vitamins	
am/pm		Minerals	
am/pm		Probiotics	
am/pm		Herbs	
am/pm		Enzymes	
am/pm		Amino Acids	

OR

time	product	description	X
am/pm	**LIVING FUEL Rx** Super Greens and/or Super Berry	Enzymes, Probiotic, Amino Acids, Herbs, Antioxidants, Vitamins and Minerals	
am/pm	**LIVING FUEL Rx** Omega 3 & E	Antioxidant protected fish oil caplets. Contains Omega 3 Fatty Acids with EPA & DHA	

Vegetables (Super Health Shopping List)

1	2	3	4	5	6	7	8

Fruits

1	2	3

Meals

time	description
am/pm	
am/pm	
am/pm	

Snacks

time	product	description	comments
am/pm			
am/pm			
am/pm			

Special Supplementation

time	product	time	product
am/pm		am/pm	
am/pm		am/pm	
am/pm		am/pm	

Exercise

cardio	time
Walk	
Running	
Biking	
Rowing	
Swimming	
Elliptical	
Other	

deep breathing exercises	minutes

strength	✓	time
7 Tiger Moves		
Additional Isoflexion. See Golden Key #3 Exercise.		
Other		
Stretching		

Stress

Be strong in the Lord and in the power of His might.—Ephesians 6:10

Sleep

Bedtime	
Wake Time	
Sleep Hours	

Environmental Toxins

Virtually every respiratory health organization lists fragrance as a trigger for asthma.

Meditation & Prayer

But you, O LORD, are a shield for me, my glory and the One who lifts up my head.—Psalm 3:3

Commitment for Tomorrow:

7 Golden Keys	Commitment
Hydration	
Nutrition	
Exercise	
Sleep	
Stress	
Environmental Toxins	
Meditation & Prayer	

day 38

date: _____

Hydration 8 oz. glasses of spring water

 1   2 3   4 5 6   7   8   9   10 11   12

Nutrition Foundation

time	source	description	X
am/pm		Protein	
am/pm		Healthy Fats	
am/pm		Fiber	
am/pm		Omega 3 EPA/DHA	
am/pm		Antioxidants	
am/pm		Vitamins	
am/pm		Minerals	
am/pm		Probiotics	
am/pm		Herbs	
am/pm		Enzymes	
am/pm		Amino Acids	

OR

time	product	description	X
am/pm	**LIVING FUEL Rx** Super Greens and/or Super Berry	Enzymes, Probiotic, Amino Acids, Herbs, Antioxidants, Vitamins and Minerals	
am/pm	**LIVING FUEL Rx** Omega 3 & E	Antioxidant protected fish oil caplets. Contains Omega 3 Fatty Acids with EPA & DHA	

Vegetables (Super Health Shopping List)

1	2	3	4	5	6	7	8

Fruits

1	2	3

Meals

time	description
am/pm	
am/pm	
am/pm	

Snacks

time	product	description	comments
am/pm			
am/pm			
am/pm			

Special Supplementation

time	product	time	product
am/pm		am/pm	
am/pm		am/pm	
am/pm		am/pm	

Exercise

cardio	time
Walk	
Running	
Biking	
Rowing	
Swimming	
Elliptical	
Other	

deep breathing exercises		minutes
strength	✓	time
7 Tiger Moves		
Additional Isoflexion. See Golden Key #3 Exercise.		
Other		
Stretching		

Stress

"I have filled him with the Spirit of God, in wisdom, in understanding, in knowledge, and in all manner of workmanship."—Exodus 31:3

Sleep

Bedtime	
Wake Time	
Sleep Hours	

Environmental Toxins

Don't cook with aluminium pots and pans or aluminium foil.

Meditation & Prayer

Bless the LORD, O my soul, and forget not all His benefits: who forgives all your iniquities, who heals all your diseases.—Psalm 103:3

Commitment for Tomorrow:

7 Golden Keys	Commitment
Hydration	
Nutrition	
Exercise	
Sleep	
Stress	
Environmental Toxins	
Meditation & Prayer	

day 39

date: _____

Hydration 8 oz. glasses of spring water

(1) (2) (3) (4) (5) (6) (7) (8) (9) (10) (11) (12)

Nutrition Foundation

time	source	description	X
am/pm		Protein	
am/pm		Healthy Fats	
am/pm		Fiber	
am/pm		Omega 3 EPA/DHA	
am/pm		Antioxidants	
am/pm		Vitamins	
am/pm		Minerals	
am/pm		Probiotics	
am/pm		Herbs	
am/pm		Enzymes	
am/pm		Amino Acids	

OR

time	product	description	X
am/pm	**LIVING FUEL Rx** Super Greens and/or Super Berry	Enzymes, Probiotic, Amino Acids, Herbs, Antioxidants, Vitamins and Minerals	
am/pm	**LIVING FUEL Rx** Omega 3 & E	Antioxidant protected fish oil caplets. Contains Omega 3 Fatty Acids with EPA & DHA	

Vegetables (Super Health Shopping List)

1	2	3	4	5	6	7	8

Fruits

1	2	3

Meals

time	description
am/pm	
am/pm	
am/pm	

Snacks

time	product	description	comments
am/pm			
am/pm			
am/pm			

Special Supplementation

time	product	time	product
am/pm		am/pm	
am/pm		am/pm	
am/pm		am/pm	

Exercise

cardio	time
Walk	
Running	
Biking	
Rowing	
Swimming	
Elliptical	
Other	

deep breathing exercises		minutes

strength	✓	time
7 Tiger Moves		
Additional Isoflexion. See Golden Key #3 Exercise.		
Other		
Stretching		

Stress

In everything give thanks; for this is the will of God in Christ Jesus for you.—1 Thessalonians 5:18

Sleep

Bedtime	
Wake Time	
Sleep Hours	

Environmental Toxins

Store meat in paper—not plastic or aluminium foil.

Meditation & Prayer

Let the words of my mouth and the meditation of my heart be acceptable in Your sight, O LORD, my strength and my Redeemer.—Psalm 19:14

Commitment for Tomorrow:

7 Golden Keys	Commitment
Hydration	
Nutrition	
Exercise	
Sleep	
Stress	
Environmental Toxins	
Meditation & Prayer	

day 39

 **day 40**

date: _____

Hydration 8 oz. glasses of spring water

(1) (2) (3) (4) (5) (6) (7) (8) (9) (10) (11) (12)

Nutrition Foundation

time	source	description	X
am/pm		Protein	
am/pm		Healthy Fats	
am/pm		Fiber	
am/pm		Omega 3 EPA/DHA	
am/pm		Antioxidants	
am/pm		Vitamins	
am/pm		Minerals	
am/pm		Probiotics	
am/pm		Herbs	
am/pm		Enzymes	
am/pm		Amino Acids	

OR

time	product	description	X
am/pm	**LIVING FUEL Rx** Super Greens and/or Super Berry	Enzymes, Probiotic, Amino Acids, Herbs, Antioxidants, Vitamins and Minerals	
am/pm	**LIVING FUEL Rx** Omega 3 & E	Antioxidant protected fish oil caplets. Contains Omega 3 Fatty Acids with EPA & DHA	

Vegetables (Super Health Shopping List)

1	2	3	4	5	6	7	8

Fruits

1	2	3

Meals

time	description
am/pm	
am/pm	
am/pm	

Snacks

time	product	description	comments
am/pm			
am/pm			
am/pm			

Special Supplementation

time	product	time	product
am/pm		am/pm	
am/pm		am/pm	
am/pm		am/pm	

Exercise

cardio	time
Walk	
Running	
Biking	
Rowing	
Swimming	
Elliptical	
Other	

deep breathing exercises		minutes
strength	✓	time
7 Tiger Moves		
Additional Isoflexion. See Golden Key #3 Exercise.		
Other		
Stretching		

Stress

The LORD is good, a stronghold in the days of trouble; and He knows those who trust in Him.—Nahum 1:7

Sleep

Bedtime	
Wake Time	
Sleep Hours	

Environmental Toxins

Use surgical steel cookware.

Meditation & Prayer

I said, "LORD, be merciful to me; heal my soul, for I have sinned against You."
—Psalm 41:4

Commitment for Tomorrow:

7 Golden Keys	Commitment
Hydration	
Nutrition	
Exercise	
Sleep	
Stress	
Environmental Toxins	
Meditation & Prayer	

day 40

 **day 41**

*date:*_____

Hydration 8 oz. glasses of spring water

 1   2 3 4   5   6   7   8   9   10   11 12

Nutrition Foundation

time	source	description	X
am/pm		Protein	
am/pm		Healthy Fats	
am/pm		Fiber	
am/pm		Omega 3 EPA/DHA	
am/pm		Antioxidants	
am/pm		Vitamins	
am/pm		Minerals	
am/pm		Probiotics	
am/pm		Herbs	
am/pm		Enzymes	
am/pm		Amino Acids	

OR

time	product	description	X
am/pm	**LIVING FUEL Rx** Super Greens and/or Super Berry	Enzymes, Probiotic, Amino Acids, Herbs, Antioxidants, Vitamins and Minerals	
am/pm	**LIVING FUEL Rx** Omega 3 & E	Antioxidant protected fish oil caplets. Contains Omega 3 Fatty Acids with EPA & DHA	

Vegetables (Super Health Shopping List)

1	2	3	4	5	6	7	8

Fruits

1	2	3

Meals

time	description
am/pm	
am/pm	
am/pm	

Snacks

time	product	description	comments
am/pm			
am/pm			
am/pm			

Special Supplementation

time	product	time	product
am/pm		am/pm	
am/pm		am/pm	
am/pm		am/pm	

Exercise

cardio	time
Walk	
Running	
Biking	
Rowing	
Swimming	
Elliptical	
Other	

deep breathing exercises	minutes

strength	✓	time
7 Tiger Moves		
Additional Isoflexion. See Golden Key #3 Exercise.		
Other		
Stretching		

Stress

He who has a slack hand becomes poor, but the hand of the diligent makes rich.—Proverbs 10:4

Sleep

Bedtime	
Wake Time	
Sleep Hours	

Environmental Toxins

Keep cold foods cold (41°F or below).

Meditation & Prayer

The LORD is my shepherd; I shall not want. He makes me to lie down in green pastures; He leads me beside the still waters. He restores my soul. —Psalm 23:1–3

Commitment for Tomorrow:

7 Golden Keys	Commitment
Hydration	
Nutrition	
Exercise	
Sleep	
Stress	
Environmental Toxins	
Meditation & Prayer	

 **day 42**   *date:* _____

Hydration   8 oz. glasses of spring water

 ① ② ③ ④ ⑤ ⑥ ⑦ ⑧ ⑨ ⑩ ⑪ ⑫

Nutrition Foundation

time	source	description	X
am/pm		Protein	
am/pm		Healthy Fats	
am/pm		Fiber	
am/pm		Omega 3 EPA/DHA	
am/pm		Antioxidants	
am/pm		Vitamins	
am/pm		Minerals	
am/pm		Probiotics	
am/pm		Herbs	
am/pm		Enzymes	
am/pm		Amino Acids	

OR

time	product	description	X
am/pm	**LIVING FUEL Rx** Super Greens and/or Super Berry	Enzymes, Probiotic, Amino Acids, Herbs, Antioxidants, Vitamins and Minerals	
am/pm	**LIVING FUEL Rx** Omega 3 & E	Antioxidant protected fish oil caplets. Contains Omega 3 Fatty Acids with EPA & DHA	

Vegetables (Super Health Shopping List)

1	2	3	4	5	6	7	8

Fruits

1	2	3

Meals

time	description
am/pm	
am/pm	
am/pm	

Snacks

time	product	description	comments
am/pm			
am/pm			
am/pm			

Special Supplementation

time	product	time	product
am/pm		am/pm	
am/pm		am/pm	
am/pm		am/pm	

Exercise

cardio	time
Walk	
Running	
Biking	
Rowing	
Swimming	
Elliptical	
Other	

deep breathing exercises		minutes
strength	✓	time
7 Tiger Moves		
Additional Isoflexion. See Golden Key #3 Exercise.		
Other		
Stretching		

Stress

Cast your burden on the LORD, and He shall sustain you; He shall never permit the righteous to be moved.—Psalm 55:22

Sleep

Bedtime	
Wake Time	
Sleep Hours	

Environmental Toxins

Avoid alcoholic beverages, corn, wheat, barley, sugar, sorghum, peanuts, rye, and cottonseed.

Meditation & Prayer

Finally, brethren, whatever things are true, whatever things are noble, whatever things are just, whatever things are pure, whatever things are lovely, whatever things are of good report, if there is any virtue and if there is anything praiseworthy—meditate on these things.—Philippians 4:8

Commitment for Tomorrow:

7 Golden Keys	Commitment
Hydration	
Nutrition	
Exercise	
Sleep	
Stress	
Environmental Toxins	
Meditation & Prayer	

day 42

week 6 summary

date: _____

7 Golden Keys	Standard	Poor	Fair	Excellent
Hydration	8–12 glasses Spring Water			
Nutrition	Four Corners Program			
Exercise	Minimum 30 minutes/day, 5–6 times/week			
Sleep	7–8.5 hours/day			
Stress	Do you feel burdened or relaxed & calm? Excellent—calm, Poor—burdened			
Environmental Toxins	Do you know the dangers & are you taking steps in your control?			
Meditation & Prayer	Excellent—daily, Poor—none			

Comments:

_____

_____

_____

_____

_____

_____

_____

_____

_____

_____

_____

_____

_____

_____

Commitment for Next Week:

_____

_____

_____

_____

_____

_____

_____

_____

_____

_____

_____

_____

Week 6

day 43

Hydration   8 oz. glasses of spring water

(1) (2) (3) (4) (5) (6) (7) (8) (9) (10) (11) (12)

Nutrition Foundation

time	source	description	X
am/pm		Protein	
am/pm		Healthy Fats	
am/pm		Fiber	
am/pm		Omega 3 EPA/DHA	
am/pm		Antioxidants	
am/pm		Vitamins	
am/pm		Minerals	
am/pm		Probiotics	
am/pm		Herbs	
am/pm		Enzymes	
am/pm		Amino Acids	

OR

time	product	description	X
am/pm	**LIVING FUEL Rx** Super Greens and/or Super Berry	Enzymes, Probiotic, Amino Acids, Herbs, Antioxidants, Vitamins and Minerals	
am/pm	**LIVING FUEL Rx** Omega 3 & E	Antioxidant protected fish oil caplets. Contains Omega 3 Fatty Acids with EPA & DHA	

Vegetables (Super Health Shopping List)

1	2	3	4	5	6	7	8

Fruits

1	2	3

Meals

time	description
am/pm	
am/pm	
am/pm	

Snacks

time	product	description	comments
am/pm			
am/pm			
am/pm			

Special Supplementation

time	product	time	product
am/pm		am/pm	
am/pm		am/pm	
am/pm		am/pm	

Exercise

cardio	time
Walk	
Running	
Biking	
Rowing	
Swimming	
Elliptical	
Other	

deep breathing exercises		minutes
strength	✓	time
7 Tiger Moves		
Additional Isoflexion. See Golden Key #3 Exercise.		
Other		
Stretching		

Stress

Commit your works to the LORD, and your thoughts will be established.
—Proverbs 16:3

Sleep

Bedtime	
Wake Time	
Sleep Hours	

Environmental Toxins

Keep the humidity level in your house below 40 percent.

Meditation & Prayer

The LORD is near to all who call on Him, to all who call upon Him in truth.
—Psalm 145:18

Commitment for Tomorrow:

7 Golden Keys	Commitment
Hydration	
Nutrition	
Exercise	
Sleep	
Stress	
Environmental Toxins	
Meditation & Prayer	

day43

 **day 44**

date: _____

Hydration 8 oz. glasses of spring water

 (1) (2) (3) (4) (5) (6) (7) (8) (9) (10) (11) (12)

Nutrition Foundation

time	source	description	X
am/pm		Protein	
am/pm		Healthy Fats	
am/pm		Fiber	
am/pm		Omega 3 EPA/DHA	
am/pm		Antioxidants	
am/pm		Vitamins	
am/pm		Minerals	
am/pm		Probiotics	
am/pm		Herbs	
am/pm		Enzymes	
am/pm		Amino Acids	

OR

time	product	description	X
am/pm	**LIVING FUEL Rx** Super Greens and/or Super Berry	Enzymes, Probiotic, Amino Acids, Herbs, Antioxidants, Vitamins and Minerals	
am/pm	**LIVING FUEL Rx** Omega 3 & E	Antioxidant protected fish oil caplets. Contains Omega 3 Fatty Acids with EPA & DHA	

Vegetables (Super Health Shopping List)

1	2	3	4	5	6	7	8

Fruits

1	2	3

Meals

time	description
am/pm	
am/pm	
am/pm	

Snacks

time	product	description	comments
am/pm			
am/pm			
am/pm			

Special Supplementation

time	product	time	product
am/pm		am/pm	
am/pm		am/pm	
am/pm		am/pm	

Exercise

cardio	time
Walk	
Running	
Biking	
Rowing	
Swimming	
Elliptical	
Other	

deep breathing exercises	minutes

strength	✓	time
7 Tiger Moves		
Additional Isoflexion. See Golden Key #3 Exercise.		
Other		
Stretching		

Stress

Casting all your care upon Him, for He cares for you.—1 Peter 5:7

Sleep

Bedtime	
Wake Time	
Sleep Hours	

Environmental Toxins

Use leftovers within three to four days so mold doesn't have an opportunity to grow.

Meditation & Prayer

Delight yourself also in the LORD, and He shall give you the desires of your heart.—Psalm 37:4

Commitment for Tomorrow:

7 Golden Keys	Commitment
Hydration	
Nutrition	
Exercise	
Sleep	
Stress	
Environmental Toxins	
Meditation & Prayer	

day 44

 **day 45**

date: _____

Hydration 8 oz. glasses of spring water

(1) (2) (3) (4) (5) (6) (7) (8) (9) (10) (11) (12)

Nutrition Foundation

time	source	description	X
am/pm		Protein	
am/pm		Healthy Fats	
am/pm		Fiber	
am/pm		Omega 3 EPA/DHA	
am/pm		Antioxidants	
am/pm		Vitamins	
am/pm		Minerals	
am/pm		Probiotics	
am/pm		Herbs	
am/pm		Enzymes	
am/pm		Amino Acids	

OR

time	product	description	X
am/pm	**LIVING FUEL Rx** Super Greens and/or Super Berry	Enzymes, Probiotic, Amino Acids, Herbs, Antioxidants, Vitamins and Minerals	
am/pm	**LIVING FUEL Rx** Omega 3 & E	Antioxidant protected fish oil caplets. Contains Omega 3 Fatty Acids with EPA & DHA	

Vegetables (Super Health Shopping List)

1	2	3	4	5	6	7	8

Fruits

1	2	3

Meals

time	description
am/pm	
am/pm	
am/pm	

Snacks

time	product	description	comments
am/pm			
am/pm			
am/pm			

Special Supplementation

time	product	time	product
am/pm		am/pm	
am/pm		am/pm	
am/pm		am/pm	

Exercise

cardio	time
Walk	
Running	
Biking	
Rowing	
Swimming	
Elliptical	
Other	

deep breathing exercises	minutes

strength	✓	time
7 Tiger Moves		
Additional Isoflexion. See Golden Key #3 Exercise.		
Other		
Stretching		

Stress

And He said, "My Presence will go with you, and I will give you rest."
—Exodus 33:14

Sleep

Bedtime	
Wake Time	
Sleep Hours	

Environmental Toxins

Install an air exchanger in your home.

Meditation & Prayer

Be anxious for nothing, but in everything by prayer and supplication, with thanksgiving, let your requests be made known to God; and the peace of God, which surpasses all understanding, will guard your hearts and minds through Christ Jesus.—Philippians 4:6–7

Commitment for Tomorrow:

7 Golden Keys	Commitment
Hydration	
Nutrition	
Exercise	
Sleep	
Stress	
Environmental Toxins	
Meditation & Prayer	

day 45

 **day 46**

date: _____

Hydration 8 oz. glasses of spring water

 (1) (2) (3) (4) (5) (6) (7) (8) (9) (10) (11) (12)

Nutrition Foundation

time	source	description	X
am/pm		Protein	
am/pm		Healthy Fats	
am/pm		Fiber	
am/pm		Omega 3 EPA/DHA	
am/pm		Antioxidants	
am/pm		Vitamins	
am/pm		Minerals	
am/pm		Probiotics	
am/pm		Herbs	
am/pm		Enzymes	
am/pm		Amino Acids	

OR

time	product	description	X
am/pm	**LIVING FUEL Rx** Super Greens and/or Super Berry	Enzymes, Probiotic, Amino Acids, Herbs, Antioxidants, Vitamins and Minerals	
am/pm	**LIVING FUEL Rx** Omega 3 & E	Antioxidant protected fish oil caplets. Contains Omega 3 Fatty Acids with EPA & DHA	

Vegetables (Super Health Shopping List)

1	2	3	4	5	6	7	8

Fruits

1	2	3

Meals

time	description
am/pm	
am/pm	
am/pm	

Snacks

time	product	description	comments
am/pm			
am/pm			
am/pm			

Special Supplementation

time	product	time	product
am/pm		am/pm	
am/pm		am/pm	
am/pm		am/pm	

Exercise

cardio	time
Walk	
Running	
Biking	
Rowing	
Swimming	
Elliptical	
Other	

deep breathing exercises		minutes

strength	✓	time
7 Tiger Moves		
Additional Isoflexion. See Golden Key #3 Exercise.		
Other		
Stretching		

Stress

"But seek first the kingdom of God and His righteous, and all these things shall be added to you."—Matthew 6:33

Sleep

Bedtime	
Wake Time	
Sleep Hours	

Environmental Toxins

Get in the habit of using garlic, oregano, and coconut, which are naturally antiparasitic and antimicrobal.

Meditation & Prayer

If any of you lacks wisdom, let him ask of God, who gives to all liberally and without reproach, and it will be given to him.—James 1:5

Commitment for Tomorrow:

7 Golden Keys	Commitment
Hydration	
Nutrition	
Exercise	
Sleep	
Stress	
Environmental Toxins	
Meditation & Prayer	

 **day 47**

date: _____

Hydration 8 oz. glasses of spring water

(1) (2) (3) (4) (5) (6) (7) (8) (9) (10) (11) (12)

Nutrition Foundation

time	source	description	X
am/pm		Protein	
am/pm		Healthy Fats	
am/pm		Fiber	
am/pm		Omega 3 EPA/DHA	
am/pm		Antioxidants	
am/pm		Vitamins	
am/pm		Minerals	
am/pm		Probiotics	
am/pm		Herbs	
am/pm		Enzymes	
am/pm		Amino Acids	

OR

time	product	description	X
am/pm	**LIVING FUEL Rx** Super Greens and/or Super Berry	Enzymes, Probiotic, Amino Acids, Herbs, Antioxidants, Vitamins and Minerals	
am/pm	**LIVING FUEL Rx** Omega 3 & E	Antioxidant protected fish oil caplets. Contains Omega 3 Fatty Acids with EPA & DHA	

Vegetables (Super Health Shopping List)

1	2	3	4	5	6	7	8

Fruits

1	2	3

Meals

time	description
am/pm	
am/pm	
am/pm	

Snacks

time	product	description	comments
am/pm			
am/pm			
am/pm			

Special Supplementation

time	product	time	product
am/pm		am/pm	
am/pm		am/pm	
am/pm		am/pm	

Exercise

cardio	time
Walk	
Running	
Biking	
Rowing	
Swimming	
Elliptical	
Other	

deep breathing exercises	minutes

strength	✓	time
7 Tiger Moves		
Additional Isoflexion. See Golden Key #3 Exercise.		
Other		
Stretching		

Stress

And let us not grow weary while doing good, for in due season we shall reap if we do not lose heart.—Galatians 6:9

Sleep

Bedtime	
Wake Time	
Sleep Hours	

Environmental Toxins

If possible, use area rugs rather than wall-to-wall carpeting.

Meditation & Prayer

In the beginning God created the heavens and the earth.—Genesis 1:1

Commitment for Tomorrow:

7 Golden Keys	Commitment
Hydration	
Nutrition	
Exercise	
Sleep	
Stress	
Environmental Toxins	
Meditation & Prayer	

day 47

 **day 48**

date: _____

Hydration 8 oz. glasses of spring water

(1) (2) (3) (4) (5) (6) (7) (8) (9) (10) (11) (12)

Nutrition Foundation

time	source	description	X
am/pm		Protein	
am/pm		Healthy Fats	
am/pm		Fiber	
am/pm		Omega 3 EPA/DHA	
am/pm		Antioxidants	
am/pm		Vitamins	
am/pm		Minerals	
am/pm		Probiotics	
am/pm		Herbs	
am/pm		Enzymes	
am/pm		Amino Acids	

OR

time	product	description	X
am/pm	**LIVING FUEL Rx** Super Greens and/or Super Berry	Enzymes, Probiotic, Amino Acids, Herbs, Antioxidants, Vitamins and Minerals	
am/pm	**LIVING FUEL Rx** Omega 3 & E	Antioxidant protected fish oil caplets. Contains Omega 3 Fatty Acids with EPA & DHA	

Vegetables (Super Health Shopping List)

1	2	3	4	5	6	7	8

Fruits

1	2	3

Meals

time	description
am/pm	
am/pm	
am/pm	

Snacks

time	product	description	comments
am/pm			
am/pm			
am/pm			

Special Supplementation

time	product	time	product
am/pm		am/pm	
am/pm		am/pm	
am/pm		am/pm	

Exercise

deep breathing exercises		minutes

cardio	time
Walk	
Running	
Biking	
Rowing	
Swimming	
Elliptical	
Other	

strength	✓	time
7 Tiger Moves		
Additional Isoflexion. See Golden Key #3 Exercise.		
Other		
Stretching		

Stress

The LORD will give strength to His people; the LORD will bless His people with peace.—Psalm 29:11

Sleep

Bedtime	
Wake Time	
Sleep Hours	

Environmental Toxins

Take potassium iodine supplements before having any medical X-rays done.

Meditation & Prayer

My people will dwell in a peaceful habitation, in secure dwellings, and in quiet resting places.—Isaiah 32:18

Commitment for Tomorrow:

7 Golden Keys	Commitment
Hydration	
Nutrition	
Exercise	
Sleep	
Stress	
Environmental Toxins	
Meditation & Prayer	

 **day 49**

date: _____

Hydration   8 oz. glasses of spring water

 1   2   3   4   5   6   7   8   9   10   11 12

Nutrition Foundation

time	source	description	X
am/pm		Protein	
am/pm		Healthy Fats	
am/pm		Fiber	
am/pm		Omega 3 EPA/DHA	
am/pm		Antioxidants	
am/pm		Vitamins	
am/pm		Minerals	
am/pm		Probiotics	
am/pm		Herbs	
am/pm		Enzymes	
am/pm		Amino Acids	

OR

time	product	description	X
am/pm	**LIVING FUEL Rx** Super Greens and/or Super Berry	Enzymes, Probiotic, Amino Acids, Herbs, Antioxidants, Vitamins and Minerals	
am/pm	**LIVING FUEL Rx** Omega 3 & E	Antioxidant protected fish oil caplets. Contains Omega 3 Fatty Acids with EPA & DHA	

Vegetables (Super Health Shopping List)

1	2	3	4	5	6	7	8

Fruits

1	2	3

Meals

time	description
am/pm	
am/pm	
am/pm	

Snacks

time	product	description	comments
am/pm			
am/pm			
am/pm			

Special Supplementation

time	product	time	product
am/pm		am/pm	
am/pm		am/pm	
am/pm		am/pm	

Exercise

cardio	time
Walk	
Running	
Biking	
Rowing	
Swimming	
Elliptical	
Other	

deep breathing exercises	minutes

strength	✓	time
7 Tiger Moves		
Additional Isoflexion. See Golden Key #3 Exercise.		
Other		
Stretching		

Stress

Monitor your bodily responses regularly—your respiration, muscular tension, and heart rate.

Sleep

Bedtime	
Wake Time	
Sleep Hours	

Environmental Toxins

Do not microwave foods. *Never microwave plastics.* Try to use your oven or stove top for all cooking purposes.

Meditation & Prayer

"Blessed are the peacemakers, for they shall be called sons of God."
—Matthew 5:9

Commitment for Tomorrow:

7 Golden Keys	Commitment
Hydration	
Nutrition	
Exercise	
Sleep	
Stress	
Environmental Toxins	
Meditation & Prayer	

day 49

week 7 summary

date: _____

7 Golden Keys	Standard	Poor	Fair	Excellent
Hydration	8–12 glasses Spring Water			
Nutrition	Four Corners Program			
Exercise	Minimum 30 minutes/day, 5–6 times/week			
Sleep	7–8.5 hours/day			
Stress	Do you feel burdened or relaxed & calm? Excellent—calm, Poor—burdened			
Environmental Toxins	Do you know the dangers & are you taking steps in your control?			
Meditation & Prayer	Excellent—daily, Poor—none			

Comments:

Commitment for Next Week:

congratulations!

WELL DONE! You have successfully completed your seven-week *Living the Seven Keys to Lifelong Vitality* program.

By now you've discovered how these simple, practical health principles can profoundly change your health, your confidence, and your overall outlook and well-being. Let's recap what you've accomplished so far!

You've made a conscious decision to treat your body as the precious temple God intended it to be.

You've set some goals, created a strategy for reaching them, and actively applied yourself to transforming bad habits into good on a daily basis.

You've learned how to replenish and feed your temple by replenishing it with pure water, nutritious foods, and regular exercise.

You've laid a strong foundation for reaching your personal dreams.

You've discovered how to nourish your spirit with rest, prayer, meditation, and a balanced lifestyle that reduces stress and helps you to avoid the toxins that compromise health and longevity.

Stay the Course!

It's important to keep forging ahead. You've accomplished great things, but as the saying goes, *this is the first day of the rest of your life.*

- Continue to adopt the "whole person" approach to health management (hydration, nutrition, exercise, stress management, sleep, avoiding environmental toxins, and meditation and prayer).

- Consciously make these priorities a part of your daily ritual, and soon they will become second nature.

- Don't overwhelm yourself by trying to do too much too fast or by setting goals that are out of reach. Apply a little of what you are learning each day and don't be discouraged by setbacks.

- Continue to take responsibility for your own health. Ask questions, read books, search for information on the Internet, talk to a trusted health professional. In short, keep learning!

- Work with an accountability partner or support group to give you that added incentive and encouragement.

- Reorder the journal keys, depending on your unique needs and priorities.

Do you have a question or concern about the program? Drop me a line at superhealth@7goldenkeys.com.

God bless,

K.C. Craichy

comprehensive nutritional chart

Food Item	Amount	Fat Grams	Calories	Carbo Grams	Protein Grams	Chol. Mgs.	Saturated Fat
1000 Island Salad Dressing	1 T	6	60	2	0	4	1
100% Natural cereal	1 oz.	6	135	18	3	0	4.1
40% Bran Flakes, Kellogg's	1 oz.	1	90	22	4	0	.1
40% Bran Flakes, Post	1 oz.	0	90	22	3	0	.1
Alfalfa seeds, sprouted, raw	1 cup	0	10	1	1	0	0
All-Bran cereal	1 oz.	1	70	21	4	0	.1
Almonds, slivered	1 cup	70	795	28	27	0	6.7
Almonds, whole	1 oz.	15	165	6	6	0	1.4
Angel Food Cake, from mix	1 piece	0	125	29	3	0	0
Apple juice, canned	1 cup	0	115	29	0	0	0
Apple pie	1 piece	18	405	60	3	0	4.6
Applesauce, canned, sweetened	1 cup	0	195	51	0	0	.1
Applesauce, canned, unsweetened	1 cup	0	105	28	0	0	0
Apples, raw, peeled, sliced	1 cup	0	65	16	0	0	.1
Apples, raw, unpeeled	1	0	80	21	0	0	.1
Apricots, canned, juice packed	1 cup	0	120	31	2	0	0
Apricots, dried, uncooked	1 cup	1	310	80	5	0	0
Apricots, raw	3	0	50	12	1	0	0
Apricot, canned, heavy syrup	1 cup	0	215	55	1	0	0
Artichokes, globe, cooked	1	0	55	12	3	0	0
Asparagus, cooked from frozen	1 cup	1	50	9	5	0	.2
Asparagus, cooked from raw	1 cup	1	45	8	5	0	.1
Asparagus, canned, spears	4 spears	0	10	2	1	0	0
Avocados, California	1	30	305	12	4	0	4.5
Avocados, Florida	1	27	340	27	5	0	5.3
Bagels, egg	1	2	200	38	7	44	.3
Bagels, plain	1	2	200	38	7	0	.3
Baking powder, low sodium	1 tsp	0	5	1	0	0	0
Baking powder, straight phosphate	1 tsp	0	5	1	0	0	0
Baking powder biscuits, from mix	1	3	95	14	2	0	.8
Baking powder biscuits, home rec.	1	5	100	13	2	0	1.2
Bamboo shoots, canned, drained	1 cup	1	25	4	2	0	.1
Bananas	1	1	105	27	1	0	.2
Bananas, sliced	1 cup	1	140	35	2	0	.3
Barbecue sauce	1 T	0	10	2	0	0	0

Food Item	Amount	Fat Grams	Calories	Carbo Grams	Protein Grams	Chol. Mgs.	Saturated Fat
Barley, pearled, light, uncooked	1 cup	2	700	158	16	0	.3
Bean sprouts, mung, cooked, drain	1 cup	0	25	5	3	0	0
Bean sprouts, mung, raw	1 cup	0	30	6	3	0	0
Bean with bacon soup, canned	1 cup	6	170	23	8	3	1.5
Beans, dry, canned, w/frankfurter	1 cup	18	365	32	19	30	7.4
Beans, dry, can., w/pork+swt. sce.	1 cup	12	385	54	16	10	4.3
Beef and vegetable stew, hm. rec.	1 cup	11	220	15	16	71	4.4
Beef broth, bouillon, cons., canned	1 cup	1	15	0	3	0	.3
Beef gravy, canned	1 cup	5	125	11	9	7	2.7
Beef heart, braised	3 oz.	5	150	0	24	164	1.2
Beef liver, fried	3 oz.	7	185	7	23	410	2.5
Beef noodle soup, canned	1 cup	3	85	9	5	5	1.1
Beef potpie, home recipe	1 piece	30	515	39	21	42	7.9
Beef roast, eye o round, lean	2.6 oz.	5	135	0	22	52	1.9
Beef roast, rib, lean only	2.2 oz.	9	150	0	17	49	3.6
Beef steak, sirloin, broil, lean	2.5 oz.	6	150	0	22	64	2.6
Beef, canned, corned	3 oz.	10	185	0	22	80	4.2
Beef, ckd., bttm. round, lean only	2.8 oz.	8	175	0	25	75	2.7
Beef, ckd., bttm. round, lean+fat	3 oz.	13	220	0	25	81	4.8
Beef, ckd., chuck blade, lean only	2.2 oz.	9	170	0	19	66	3.9
Beef, ckd., chuck blade, lean+fat	3 oz.	26	325	0	22	87	10.8
Beef, dried, chipped	2.5 oz.	4	145	0	24	46	1.8
Beer, light	12 F oz.	0	95	5	1	0	0
Beer, regular	12 F oz.	0	150	13	1	0	0
Beet greens, cooked, drained	1 cup	0	40	8	4	0	0
Beets, canned, drained	1 cup	0	55	12	2	0	0
Beets, cooked, drained, diced	1 cup	0	55	11	2	0	0
Beets, cooked, drained, whole	2 beets	0	30	7	1	0	0
Black beans, dry, cooked, drained	1 cup	1	225	41	15	0	.1
Blackberries, raw	1 cup	1	75	18	1	0	.2
Black-eyed peas, dry, cooked	1 cup	1	190	35	13	0	.2
Black-eyed peas, raw, cooked	1 cup	1	180	30	13	0	.3
Black-eyed peas, frzn., cooked	1 cup	1	225	40	14	0	.3
Blue cheese	1 oz.	8	100	1	6	21	5.3
Blue cheese salad dressing	1 T	8	75	1	1	3	1.5
Blueberries, frozen, sweetened	1 cup	0	185	50	1	0	0
Blueberries, raw	1 cup	1	80	20	1	0	0
Blueberry muffins, home recipe	1	5	135	20	3	19	1.5
Blueberry pie	1 piece	17	380	55	4	0	4.3
Bologna	2 slices	16	180	2	7	31	6.1
Boston brown bread	1 slice	1	95	21	2	3	.3
Bouillon, dehydrated, unprepared	1 pkt	1	15	1	1	1	.3
Bran muffins, home recipe	1	6	125	19	3	24	1.4

Food Item	Amount	Fat Grams	Calories	Carbo Grams	Protein Grams	Chol. Mgs.	Saturated Fat
Braunschweiger	2 slices	18	205	2	8	89	6.2
Brazil nuts	1 oz.	19	185	4	4	0	4.6
Bread stuffing, from mix, dry type	1 cup	31	500	50	9	0	6.1
Bread stuffing, from mix, moist	1 cup	26	420	40	9	67	5.3
Breadcrumbs, dry, grated	1 cup	5	390	73	13	5	1.5
Broccoli, frozen, cooked, drained	1 cup	0	50	10	6	0	0
Broccoli, raw	1 spear	1	40	8	4	0	.1
Broccoli, raw, cooked, drained	1 cup	0	45	9	5	0	.1
Brown and serve sausage	1 link	5	50	0	2	9	1.7
Brown gravy from dry mix	1 cup	2	80	14	3	2	.9
Brownies w/nuts, home recipe	1 sq.	6	95	11	1	18	1.4
Brussels sprouts, frozen, cooked	1 cup	1	65	13	6	0	.1
Brussels sprouts, raw, cooked	1 cup	1	60	13	4	0	.2
Buckwheat flour, light, sifted	1 cup	1	340	78	6	0	.2
Bulgur, uncooked	1 cup	3	600	129	19	0	1.2
Buttermilk, dried	1 cup	7	465	59	41	83	4.3
Buttermilk, fluid	1 cup	2	100	12	8	9	1.3
Butter	1 pat	4	35	0	0	11	2.5
Butter	1 T	11	100	0	0	31	7.1
Cabbage, Chinese, pak-choi, ckd.	1 cup	0	20	3	3	0	0
Cabbage, Chinese, pe-tsai, raw	1 cup	0	10	2	1	0	0
Cabbage, common, cooked	1 cup	0	30	7	1	0	0
Cabbage, common, raw	1 cup	0	15	4	1	0	0
Cabbage, red, raw	1 cup	0	20	4	1	0	0
Cabbage, savoy, raw	1 cup	0	20	4	1	0	0
Cake or pastry flour, sifted	1 cup	1	350	76	7	0	.1
Camembert cheese	1 wedge	9	115	0	8	27	5.8
Cantaloupe, raw	1/2	1	95	22	2	0	.1
Captain Crunch cereal	1 oz.	3	120	23	1	0	1.7
Caramels, plain or chocolate	1 oz.	3	115	22	1	1	2.2
Carob flour	1 cup	0	255	126	6	0	0
Carrot cake, cream cheese frosting	1 piece	21	385	48	4	74	4.1
Carrots, canned	1 cup	0	35	8	1	0	.1
Carrots, cooked, frozen	1 cup	0	55	12	2	0	0
Carrots, cooked, raw	1 cup	0	70	16	2	0	.1
Cashew nuts, dry roasted	1 oz.	13	165	9	4	0	2.6
Cashew nuts, oil roasted	1 oz.	14	165	8	5	0	2.7
Catsup	1 T	0	15	4	0	0	0
Cauliflower, cooked from frozen	1 cup	0	35	7	3	0	.1
Cauliflower, cooked from raw	1 cup	0	30	6	2	0	0
Cauliflower, raw	1 cup	0	25	5	2	0	0
Celery seed	1 tsp	1	10	1	0	0	0
Celery, pascal type, raw, piece	1 cup	0	20	4	1	0	0

Food Item	Amount	Fat Grams	Calories	Carbo Grams	Protein Grams	Chol. Mgs.	Saturated Fat
Cheddar cheese	1 cu. in.	6	70	0	4	18	3.6
Cheddar cheese	1 oz.	9	115	0	7	30	6
Cheddar cheese, shredded	1 cup	37	455	1	28	119	23.8
Cheerios cereal	1 oz.	2	110	20	4	0	.3
Cheese crackers, plain	10	3	50	6	1	6	.9
Cheese sauce w/milk, from mix	1 cup	17	305	23	16	53	9.3
Cheeseburger, 4 oz. patty	1	31	525	40	30	104	15.1
Cheesecake	1 piece	18	280	26	5	170	9.9
Cherries, sour, red, canned, water	1 cup	0	90	22	2	0	.1
Cherries, sweet, raw	10	1	50	11	1	0	.1
Cherry pie	1 piece	18	410	61	4	0	4.7
Chestnuts, European, roasted	1 cup	3	350	76	5	0	.6
Chicken a la king, home recipe	1 cup	34	470	12	27	221	12.9
Chicken and noodles, home recipe	1 cup	18	365	26	22	103	5.1
Chicken chow mein, canned	1 cup	0	95	18	7	8	.1
Chicken chow mein, home recipe	1 cup	10	255	10	31	75	4.1
Chicken frankfurter	1	9	115	3	6	45	2.5
Chicken gravy from dry mix	1 cup	2	85	14	3	3	.5
Chicken gravy, canned	1 cup	14	190	13	5	5	3.4
Chicken liver, cooked	1	1	30	0	5	126	.4
Chicken noodle soup, canned	1 cup	2	75	9	4	7	.7
Chicken noodle soup, dehyd.	1 pkt	1	40	6	2	2	.2
Chicken potpie, home recipe	1 piece	31	545	42	23	56	10.3
Chicken rice soup, canned	1 cup	2	60	7	4	7	.5
Chicken roll, light	2 slices	4	90	1	11	28	1.1
Chicken, canned, boneless	5 oz.	11	235	0	31	88	3.1
Chicken, fried, batter, breast	4.9 oz.	18	365	13	35	119	4.9
Chicken, fried, batter, drumstick	2.5 oz.	11	195	6	16	62	3
Chicken, fried, flour, breast	3.5 oz.	9	220	2	31	87	2.4
Chicken, fried, flour, drumstick	1.7 oz.	7	120	1	13	44	1.8
Chicken, roasted, breast	3 oz.	3	140	0	27	73	.9
Chicken, roasted, drumstick	1.6 oz.	2	75	0	12	41	.7
Chicken, stewed, light + dark	1 cup	9	250	0	38	116	2.6
Chickpeas, cooked, drained	1 cup	4	270	45	15	0	.4
Chili con carne w/beans, canned	1 cup	16	340	31	19	28	5.8
Chili powder	1 tsp	0	10	1	0	0	.1
Chocolate chip cookies	4	11	185	26	2	18	3.9
Chocolate chip cookies, refrig.	4	11	225	32	2	22	4
Chocolate milk, low-fat 1%	1 cup	3	160	26	8	7	1.5
Chocolate milk, low-fat 2%	1 cup	5	180	26	8	17	3.1
Chocolate milk, regular	1 cup	8	210	26	8	31	5.3
Chocolate, bitter	1 oz.	15	145	8	3	0	9
Chip suey w/beef + pork, home rec.	1 cup	17	300	13	26	68	4.3

Food Item	Amount	Fat Grams	Calories	Carbo Grams	Protein Grams	Chol. Mgs.	Saturated Fat
Cinnamon	1 tsp	0	5	2	0	0	0
Clam chowder, Manhattan, canned	1 cup	2	80	12	4	2	.4
Clam chowder, New Eng., w/milk	1 cup	7	165	17	9	22	3
Clams, canned, drained	3 oz.	2	85	2	13	54	.5
Clams, raw	3 oz.	1	65	2	11	43	.3
Club soda	12 F oz.	0	0	0	0	0	0
Cocoa pwdr. w/o no-fat dry milk	1 serv.	9	225	30	9	33	5.4
Cocoa pwdr. w/no-fat dry milk	1 serv.	1	100	22	3	1	.6
Coconut, dried, sweet., shredded	1 cup	33	470	44	3	0	29.3
Coconut, raw, piece	1 piece	15	160	7	1	0	13.4
Coconut, raw, shredded	1 cup	27	285	12	3	0	23.8
Coffee cake, crumb, from mix	1 piece	7	230	38	5	47	2
Coffee, brewed	6 F oz.	0	0	0	0	0	0
Coffee, instant, prepared	6 F oz.	0	0	1	0	0	0
Cola, diet, aspartame only	12 F oz.	0	0	0	0	0	0
Cola, diet, saccharin only	12 F oz.	0	0	0	0	0	0
Cola, regular	12 F oz.	0	160	41	0	0	0
Collards, cooked from frozen	1 cup	1	60	12	5	0	.1
Collards, cooked from raw	1 cup	0	25	5	2	0	.1
Cooked salad dressing, home rec.	1 T	2	25	2	1	9	.5
Corn chips	1 oz.	9	155	16	2	0	1.4
Corn Flakes, Kellogg's	1 oz.	0	110	24	2	0	0
Corn grits, cooked, instant	1 pkt	0	80	18	2	0	0
Corn grits, ckd., yellow or white	1 cup	0	145	31	3	0	0
Corn muffins, home recipe	1	5	145	21	3	23	1.5
Corn oil	1 T	14	125	0	0	0	1.8
Cornmeal, bolted, dry form	1 cup	4	440	91	11	0	.5
Cornmeal, degermed, enriched, ck.	1 cup	0	120	26	3	0	0
Cornmeal, degermed, enriched, dry	1 cup	2	500	108	11	0	.2
Cornmeal, whole-grnd., unbolt, dry	1 cup	5	435	90	11	0	.5
Corn, canned, cream style, white	1 cup	1	185	46	4	0	.2
Corn, canned, cream style, yellow	1 cup	1	185	46	4	0	.2
Corn, cooked from frozen, white	1 cup	0	135	34	5	0	0
Corn, cooked from frozen, white	1 ear	0	60	14	2	0	.1
Corn, cooked from frozen, yellow	1 cup	0	135	34	5	0	0
Corn, cooked from frozen, yellow	1 ear	0	60	14	2	0	.1
Corn, cooked from raw, white	1 ear	1	85	19	3	0	.2
Corn, cooked from raw, yellow	1 ear	1	85	19	3	0	.2
Corn, canned, whole kernel, white	1 cup	1	165	41	5	0	.2
Corn, canned, whole kernel, yellow	1 cup	1	165	41	5	0	.2
Cottage cheese, cr., large curd	1 cup	10	235	6	28	34	6.4
Cottage cheese, cr., w/fruit	1 cup	8	280	30	22	25	4.9
Cottage cheese, low-fat 2%	1 cup	4	205	8	31	19	2.8

Food Item	Amount	Fat Grams	Calories	Carbo Grams	Protein Grams	Chol. Mgs.	Saturated Fat
Cottage cheese, uncreamed	1 cup	1	125	3	25	10	.4
Cream of chicken soup w/water	1 cup	7	115	9	3	10	2.1
Cream of chicken soup w/milk	1 cup	11	190	15	7	27	4.6
Cream of mushroom soup w/water	1 cup	9	130	9	2	2	2.4
Cream of mushroom soup w/milk	1 cup	14	205	15	6	20	5.1
Crabmeat, canned	1 cup	3	135	1	23	135	.5
Cracked-wheat bread	1 slice	1	65	12	2	0	.2
Cranberry juice cocktail	1 cup	0	145	38	0	0	0
Cranberry sauce, canned, swtnd.	1 cup	0	420	108	1	0	0
Cream cheese	1 oz.	10	100	1	2	31	6.2
Cream of Wheat, cooked	1 pkt	0	100	21	3	0	0
Crème pie	1 piece	23	455	59	3	8	15
Creamed wheat, cooked	1 cup	0	140	29	4	0	.1
Croissants	1	12	235	27	5	13	3.5
Cucumber, w/peel	6 slices	0	5	1	0	0	0
Curry powder	1 tsp	0	5	1	0	0	0
Custard pie	1 piece	17	330	36	9	169	5.6
Custard, baked	1 cup	15	305	29	14	278	6.8
Dandelion, cooked, drained	1 cup	1	35	7	2	0	.1
Danish pastry, fruit	1	13	235	28	4	56	3.9
Danish pastry, plain, no nuts	1	12	220	26	4	49	3.6
Dates, chopped	1 cup	1	490	131	4	0	.3
Devil's Food Cake, frst., cupcake	1	4	120	20	2	19	1.8
Doughnuts, cake type, plain	1	12	210	24	3	20	2.8
Doughnuts, yeast-leavened, glazed	1	13	235	26	4	21	5.2
Duck, roasted, flesh only	1/2 duck	25	445	0	52	197	9.2
Eggnog	1 cup	19	340	34	10	149	11.3
Eggplant, cooked, steamed	1 cup	0	25	6	1	0	0
Eggs, cooked, fried	1	7	90	1	6	211	1.9
Eggs, cooked, hard-cooked	1	5	75	1	6	213	1.6
Eggs, cooked, poached	1	5	75	1	6	212	1.5
Eggs, cooked, scrambled/omelet	1	7	100	1	7	215	2.2
Eggs, raw, white	1	0	15	0	4	0	0
Eggs, raw, whole	1	5	75	1	6	213	1.6
Eggs, raw, yolk	1	5	60	0	3	213	1.6
Enchilada	1	6	235	24	20	19	7.7
Endive, curly, raw	1 cup	0	10	2	1	0	0
English muffin, egg, cheese, bacon	1	18	360	31	18	213	8
English muffins, plain	1	1	140	27	5	0	.3
Evaporated milk, skim, canned	1 cup	1	200	29	19	9	.3
Evaporated milk, whole, canned	1 cup	19	340	25	17	74	11.6
Fats, cooking/vegetable shortening	1 T	13	115	0	0	0	3.3
Feta cheese	1 oz.	6	75	1	4	25	4.2

Food Item	Amount	Fat Grams	Calories	Carbo Grams	Protein Grams	Chol. Mgs.	Saturated Fat
Fig bars	4	4	210	42	2	27	1
Figs, dried	10	2	475	122	6	0	.4
Filberts, (hazelnuts) chopped	1 cup	72	725	18	15	0	5.3
Fish sandwich, large, w/o cheese	1	27	470	41	18	91	6.3
Fish sandwich, regular, w/cheese	1	23	420	39	16	56	6.3
Fish sticks, frozen, reheated	1 stick	3	70	4	6	26	.8
Flounder or sole, baked, butter	3 oz.	6	120	0	16	68	3.2
Flounder or sole, baked, w/o fat	3 oz.	1	80	0	17	59	.3
Fondant, uncoated	1 oz.	0	105	27	0	0	0
Frankfurter, cooked	1	13	145	1	5	23	4.8
French bread	1 slice	1	100	18	3	0	.3
French salad dressing, low calorie	1 T	2	25	2	0	0	.2
French salad dressing, regular	1 T	9	85	1	0	0	1.4
French toast, home recipe	1 slice	7	155	17	6	112	1.6
Fried pie, apple	1 pie	14	255	31	2	14	5.8
Fried pie, cherry	1 pie	14	250	32	2	13	5.8
Froot Loops cereal	1 oz.	1	110	25	2	0	.2
Fruit cocktail, heavy syrup	1 cup	0	185	48	1	0	0
Fruit cocktail, juice packed	1 cup	0	115	29	1	0	0
Fruit punch drink, canned	6 F oz.	0	85	22	0	0	0
Fruitcake, dark, from home recipe	1 piece	7	165	25	2	20	1.5
Fudge, chocolate, plain	1 oz.	3	115	21	1	1	2.1
Garlic powder	1 tsp	0	10	2	0	0	0
Gelatin dessert, prepared	1/2 cup	0	70	17	2	0	0
Gelatin, dry	1 env.	0	25	0	6	0	0
Ginger ale	12 F oz.	0	125	32	0	0	0
Gingerbread cake, from mix	1 piece	4	175	32	2	1	1.1
Gin/rum/vodka/whiskey 80-proof	1.5 F oz.	0	95	0	0	0	0
Gin/rum/vodka/whiskey 90-proof	1.5 F oz.	0	110	0	0	0	0
Golden Grahams cereal	1 oz.	1	110	24	2	0	.7
Graham cracker, plain	2	1	60	11	1	0	.4
Grape-Nuts cereal	1 oz.	0	100	23	3	0	0
Grape drink, canned	6 F oz.	0	100	26	0	0	0
Grape juice, canned	1 cup	0	155	38	1	0	.1
Grape soda	12 F oz.	0	180	46	0	0	0
Grapefruit j., frzn., conc., unswten.	6 F oz.	1	300	72	4	0	.1
Grapefruit juice, canned, unswten.	1 cup	0	95	22	1	0	0
Grapefruit juice, raw	1 cup	0	95	23	1	0	0
Grapefruit, canned, syrup pack	1 cup	0	150	39	1	0	0
Grapefruit, raw, pink or white	1/2 fruit	0	40	10	1	0	0
Grape juice, frzn., conc., swten.	6 F oz.	1	385	96	1	0	.2
Grapes, European, raw, Thompson	10	0	35	9	0	0	.1
Gravy and turkey, frozen	5 oz.	4	95	7	8	26	1.2

Food Item	Amount	Fat Grams	Calories	Carbo Grams	Protein Grams	Chol. Mgs.	Saturated Fat
Great northern beans, dry, cooked	1 cup	1	210	38	14	0	.1
Ground beef, broiled, lean	3 oz.	16	230	0	21	74	6.2
Ground beef, broiled, regular	3 oz.	18	245	0	20	76	6.9
Gum drops	1 oz.	0	100	25	0	0	0
Haddock, breaded, fried	3 oz.	9	175	7	17	75	2.4
Half and half, cream	1 cup	28	315	10	7	89	17.3
Halibut, broiled, butter, lemon j.	3 oz.	6	140	0	20	62	3.3
Hamburger, 4 oz. patty	1	21	445	38	25	71	7.1
Hamburger, regular	1	11	245	28	12	32	4.4
Hard candy	1 oz.	0	110	28	0	0	0
Herring, pickled	3 oz.	13	190	0	17	85	4.3
Hollandaise sauce from mix	1 cup	20	240	14	5	52	11.6
Honey	1 T	0	65	17	0	0	0
Honey Nut Cheerios cereal	1 oz.	1	105	23	3	0	.1
Honeydew melon, raw	1/10	0	45	12	1	0	0
Ice cream, vanilla, regular 11% fat	1 cup	14	270	32	5	59	8.9
Ice cream, vanilla, rich 16% fat	1 cup	24	350	32	4	88	14.7
Ice cream, vanilla, soft serve	1 cup	23	375	38	7	153	13.5
Ice milk, vanilla, 4% fat	1 cup	6	185	29	5	18	3.5
Ice milk, vanilla, soft serve 3% fat	1 cup	5	225	38	8	13	2.9
Imitation creamers, liquid frozen	1 T	1	20	2	0	0	1.4
Imitation creamers, powdered	1 tsp	1	10	1	0	0	.7
Imitation whipped topping, frz.	1 T	1	15	1	0	0	.9
Imitation sour dressing	1 T	2	20	1	0	1	1.6
Imitation whipped topping	1 T	1	10	1	0	0	.8
Italian bread	1 slice	0	85	17	3	0	0
Italian salad dressing, low calorie	1 T	0	5	2	0	0	0
Italian salad dressing, regular	1 T	9	80	1	0	0	1.3
Jams and preserves	1 T	0	55	14	0	0	0
Jellies	1 T	0	50	13	0	0	0
Jelly beans	1 oz.	0	105	26	0	0	0
Jerusalem-artichoke, raw	1 cup	0	115	26	3	0	0
Kale, cooked from frozen	1 cup	1	40	7	4	0	.1
Kale, cooked from raw	1 cup	1	40	7	2	0	.1
Kiwifruit, raw	1	0	45	11	1	0	0
Kohlrabi, cooked, drained	1 cup	0	50	11	3	0	0
Lamb, rib, roasted, lean only	2 oz.	7	130	0	15	50	3.2
Lamb, chops, arm, braised, lean	1.7 oz.	7	135	0	17	59	2.9
Lamb, chops, loin, broil, lean	2.3 oz.	6	140	0	19	60	2.6
Lamb, leg, roasted, lean only	2.6 oz.	6	140	0	20	65	2.4
Lard	1 T	13	115	0	0	12	5.1
Lemon-lime soda	12 F oz.	0	155	39	0	0	0
Lemon juice, canned	1 T	0	5	1	0	0	0

Food Item	Amount	Fat Grams	Calories	Carbo Grams	Protein Grams	Chol. Mgs.	Saturated Fat
Lemon juice, raw	1 cup	0	60	21	1	0	0
Lemon juice, frzn., single-strength	6 F oz.	1	55	16	1	0	.1
Lemon meringue pie	1 piece	14	355	53	5	143	4.3
Lemonade, concentrate, fzn., undil.	6 F oz.	0	425	112	0	0	0
Lemons, raw	1 lemon	0	15	5	1	0	0
Lentils, dry, cooked	1 cup	1	215	38	16	0	.1
Lettuce, butterhead, raw, head	1 head	0	20	4	2	0	0
Lettuce, crisphead, raw, head	1 head	1	70	11	5	0	.1
Lettuce, crisphead, raw, pieces	1 cup	0	5	1	1	0	0
Lettuce, looseleaf	1 cup	0	10	2	1	0	0
Light, coffee or table cream	1 T	3	30	1	0	10	1.8
Lima beans, dry, cooked	1 cup	1	260	49	16	0	.2
Lima beans, baby, frzn., ckd.	1 cup	1	190	35	12	0	.1
Lima beans, thick seed, frzn., ckd.	1 cup	1	170	32	10	0	.1
Lime juice, raw	1 cup	0	65	22	1	0	0
Lime juice, canned	1 cup	1	50	16	1	0	.1
Limeade, concentrate, frzn., undil.	6 F oz.	0	410	108	0	0	0
Lucky Charms cereal	1 oz.	1	110	23	3	0	.2
Macadamia nuts, oil roasted	1 oz.	22	205	4	2	0	3.2
Macaroni and cheese, canned	1 cup	10	230	26	9	24	4.7
Macaroni and cheese, home recipe	1 cup	22	430	40	17	44	9.8
Macaroni, cooked, firm	1 cup	1	190	39	7	0	.1
Malt-O-Meal	1 cup	0	120	26	4	0	0
Malted milk, chocolate, powder	3/4 oz.	1	85	18	1	1	.5
Malted milk, natural, powder	3/4 oz.	2	85	15	3	4	.9
Mangos, raw	1	1	135	35	1	0	.1
Margarine, imitation 40% fat	1 T	5	50	0	0	0	1.1
Margarine, regular, hard, 80% fat	1 T	11	100	0	0	0	2.2
Margarine, regular, soft, 80% fat	1 T	11	100	0	0	0	1.9
Margarine, spread, hard, 60% fat	1 T	9	75	0	0	0	2
Margarine, spread, soft, 60% fat	1 T	9	75	0	0	0	1.8
Marshmallows	1 oz.	0	90	23	1	0	0
Mayonnaise type salad dressing	1 T	5	60	4	0	4	.7
Mayonnaise, regular	1 T	11	100	0	0	8	1.7
Melba toast, plain	1 piece	0	20	4	1	0	.1
Milk chocolate candy, plain	1 oz.	9	145	16	2	6	5.4
Milk chocolate candy, w/almond	1 oz.	10	150	15	3	5	4.8
Milk chocolate candy, w/peanuts	1 oz.	11	155	13	4	5	4.2
Milk chocolate candy, w/rice crpy.	1 oz.	7	140	18	2	6	4.4
Milk, low-fat, 1%, no added solid	1 cup	3	100	12	8	10	1.6
Milk, low-fat, 2%, no added solid	1 cup	5	120	12	8	18	2.9
Milk, skim, no added milk solid	1 cup	0	85	12	8	4	.3
Milk, whole, 3.3% fat	1 cup	8	150	11	8	33	5.1

Food Item	Amount	Fat Grams	Calories	Carbo Grams	Protein Grams	Chol. Mgs.	Saturated Fat
Minestrone soup, canned	1 cup	3	80	11	4	2	.6
Miso soup	1 cup	13	470	65	29	0	1.8
Mixed grain bread	1 slice	1	65	12	2	0	.2
Mixed nuts w/peanuts, dry	1 oz.	15	170	7	5	0	2
Mixed nuts w/peanuts, oil	1 oz.	16	175	6	5	0	2.5
Molasses, cane, blackstrap	2 T	0	85	22	0	0	0
Mozzarella cheese, whole milk	1 oz.	6	80	1	6	22	3.7
Mozzarella cheese, skim, lo-moist.	1 oz.	5	80	1	8	15	3.1
Muenster cheese	1 oz.	9	105	0	7	27	5.4
Mushroom gravy, canned	1 cup	6	120	13	3	0	1
Mushrooms, canned	1 cup	0	35	8	3	0	.1
Mushrooms, cooked	1 cup	1	40	8	3	0	.1
Mushrooms, raw	1 cup	0	20	3	1	0	0
Mustard greens, cooked	1 cup	0	20	3	3	0	0
Mustard, prepared, yellow	1 tsp	0	5	0	0	0	0
Nature Valley Granola cereal	1 oz.	5	125	19	3	0	3.3
Nectarines, raw	1	1	65	16	1	0	.1
Nonfat dry milk, instantized	1 cup	0	245	35	24	12	.3
Nonfat dry milk, instantized	1 env.	1	325	47	32	17	.4
Noodles, chow mein, canned	1 cup	11	220	26	6	5	2.1
Noodles, egg, cooked	1 cup	2	200	37	7	50	.5
Oatmeal bread	1 slice	1	65	12	2	0	.2
Oatmeal w/raisins cookies	4	10	245	36	3	2	2.5
Oatmeal, cooked, flavored, instant	1 pkt	2	160	31	5	0	.3
Oatmeal, cooked, plain, instant	1 pkt	2	105	18	4	0	.3
Oatmeal, cooked, rg., qck., instant	1 cup	2	145	25	6	0	.4
Ocean perch, breaded, fried	1 fillet	11	185	7	16	66	2.6
Okra pods, cooked	8 pods	0	25	6	2	0	0
Olive oil	1 cup	216	1910	0	0	0	29.2
Olive oil	1 T	14	125	0	0	0	1.9
Olives, canned, green	4 med.	2	15	0	0	0	.2
Olives, canned, ripe, mission	3 small	2	15	0	0	0	.3
Onion powder	1 tsp	0	5	2	0	0	0
Onion rings, breaded, frozen	2 rings	5	80	8	1	0	1.7
Onion soup, dehydrated	1 pkt	0	20	4	1	0	.1
Onions, raw, chopped	1 cup	0	55	12	2	0	.1
Onions, raw, cooked, drained	1 cup	0	60	13	2	0	.1
Onions, raw, sliced	1 cup	0	40	8	1	0	.1
Onions, spring, raw	6	0	10	2	1	0	0
Orange juice, canned	1 cup	0	105	25	1	0	0
Orange juice, raw	1 cup	0	110	26	2	0	.1
Orange juice, frozen, concentrate	6 F oz.	0	340	81	5	0	.1
Orange juice, frozen, concentrate	1 cup	0	110	27	2	0	0

Food Item	Amount	Fat Grams	Calories	Carbo Grams	Protein Grams	Chol. Mgs.	Saturated Fat
Orange soda	12 F oz.	0	180	46	0	0	0
Orange + grapefruit juice, canned	1 cup	0	105	25	1	0	0
Oranges, raw	1	0	60	15	1	0	0
Oranges, raw, sections	1 cup	0	85	21	2	0	0
Oregano	1 tsp	0	5	1	0	0	0
Oysters, breaded, fried	1 oyster	5	90	5	5	35	1.4
Oysters, raw	1 cup	4	160	8	20	120	1.4
Pancakes, buckwheat	1	2	55	6	2	20	.9
Pancakes, plain	1	2	60	9	2	16	.5
Papayas, raw	1 cup	0	65	17	1	0	.1
Paprika	1 tsp	0	5	1	0	0	0
Parmesan cheese, grated	1 cup	30	455	4	42	79	19.1
Parmesan cheese, grated	1 oz.	9	130	1	12	22	5.4
Parmesan cheese, grated	1 T	2	25	0	2	4	1
Parsley, freeze-dried	1 T	0	0	0	0	0	0
Parsley, raw	10 sprig	0	5	1	0	0	0
Parsnips, cooked, drained	1 cup	0	125	30	2	0	.1
Pasteurized process cheese, Swiss	1 oz.	7	95	1	7	24	4.5
Pasteurized proc. cheese, American	1 oz.	9	105	0	6	27	5.6
Pasteurized proc. ch. spread, Am.	1 oz.	6	80	2	5	16	3.8
Pea beans, dry, cooked	1 cup	1	225	40	15	0	.1
Peach pie	1 piece	17	405	60	4	0	4.1
Peaches, canned, heavy syrup	1 cup	0	190	51	1	0	0
Peaches, canned, heavy syrup	1 half	0	60	16	0	0	0
Peaches, canned, juice pack	1 cup	0	110	29	2	0	0
Peaches, canned, juice pack	1 half	0	35	9	0	0	0
Peaches, dried	1 cup	1	380	98	6	0	.1
Peaches, dried, cooked, unsweet.	1 cup	1	200	51	3	0	.1
Peaches, frozen, sweetened	1 cup	0	235	60	2	0	0
Peaches, frozen, sweetened	10 oz.	0	265	68	2	0	0
Peaches, raw	1	0	35	10	1	0	0
Peaches, raw, sliced	1 cup	0	75	19	1	0	0
Peanut butter	1 T	8	95	3	5	0	1.4
Peanut butter cookie	4	14	245	28	4	22	4
Peanut oil	1 cup	216	1910	0	0	0	36.5
Peanut oil	1 T	14	125	0	0	0	2.4
Peanuts, oil roasted	1 cup	71	840	27	39	0	9.9
Peanuts, oil roasted	1 oz.	14	165	5	8	0	1.9
Pears, canned, heavy syrup	1 cup	0	190	49	1	0	0
Pears, canned, heavy syrup	1 half	0	60	15	0	0	0
Pears, canned, juice pack	1 cup	0	125	32	1	0	0
Pears, canned, juice pack	1 half	0	40	10	0	0	0
Pears, raw, bartlett	1	1	100	25	1	0	0

Food Item	Amount	Fat Grams	Calories	Carbo Grams	Protein Grams	Chol. Mgs.	Saturated Fat
Pears, raw, bosc	1	1	85	21	1	0	0
Pears, raw, d'anjou	1	1	120	30	1	0	0
Peas, edible pod, cooked	1 cup	0	65	11	5	0	.1
Peas, green, canned	1 cup	1	115	21	8	0	.1
Peas, split, dry, cooked	1 cup	1	230	42	16	0	.1
Peas, green, frozen, cooked	1 cup	0	125	23	8	0	.1
Pea, green, soup, canned	1 cup	3	165	27	9	0	1.4
Pecan pie	1 piece	32	575	71	7	95	4.7
Pecans, halves	1 cup	73	720	20	8	0	5.9
Pecans, halves	1 oz.	19	190	5	2	0	1.5
Peppers, hot chili, raw, red or gr.	1	0	20	4	1	0	0
Peppers, sweet, cooked, red or gr.	1	0	15	3	0	0	0
Peppers, sweet, raw, red or green	1	0	20	4	1	0	0
Pepper, black	1 tsp	0	5	1	0	0	0
Pickles, cucumber, dill	1	0	5	1	0	0	0
Pickles, cucumber, fresh pack	2 slices	0	10	3	0	0	0
Pickles, cucumber, swt. Gherkin	1 pickle	0	20	5	0	0	0
Pie crust from mix	2 crust	93	1485	141	20	0	22.7
Pie crust from home recipe	1 shell	60	900	79	11	0	14.8
Pine nuts	1 oz.	17	160	5	3	0	2.7
Pineapple-grapefruit juice drink	6 F oz.	0	90	23	0	0	0
Pineapple, canned, unsweetened	1 cup	0	140	34	1	0	0
Pineapple, canned, heavy syrup	1 cup	0	200	52	1	0	0
Pineapple, canned, heavy syrup	1 slice	0	45	12	0	0	0
Pineapple, canned, juice pack	1 cup	0	150	39	1	0	0
Pineapple, canned, juice pack	1 slice	0	35	9	0	0	0
Pineapple, raw, diced	1 cup	1	75	19	1	0	0
Pinto beans, dry, cooked, drained	1 cup	1	265	49	15	0	.1
Pistachio nuts	1 oz.	14	165	7	6	0	1.7
Pita bread	1 pita	1	165	33	6	0	.1
Pizza, cheese	1 slice	9	290	39	15	56	4.1
Plantains, cooked	1 cup	0	180	48	1	0	.1
Plantains, raw	1	1	220	57	2	0	.3
Plums, canned, heavy syrup	1 cup	0	230	60	1	0	0
Plums, canned, juice pack	1 cup	0	145	38	1	0	0
Plums, raw, 1-1/2" diameter	1	0	15	4	0	0	0
Plums, raw, 2-1/8" diameter	1	0	35	9	1	0	0
Popcorn, air-popped, unsalted	1 cup	0	30	6	1	0	0
Popcorn, popped, veg., oil, salted	1 cup	3	55	6	1	0	.5
Popcorn, sugar syrup coated	1 cup	1	135	30	2	0	.1
Popsicle	1	0	70	18	0	0	0
Pork chop, loin, broil, lean	2.5 oz.	8	165	0	23	71	2.6
Pork chop, loin, broil, lean + fat	3.1 oz.	19	275	0	24	84	7

Food Item	Amount	Fat Grams	Calories	Carbo Grams	Protein Grams	Chol. Mgs.	Saturated Fat
Pork chop, loin, panfry, lean	2.4 oz.	11	180	0	19	72	3.7
Pork chop, loin, panfry, lean + fat	3.1 oz.	27	335	0	21	92	9.8
Pork fresh ham, roasted, lean	2.5 oz.	8	160	0	20	68	2.7
Pork fresh ham, roasted, lean + fat	3 oz.	18	250	0	21	79	6.4
Pork fresh rib, roasted, lean	2.5 oz.	10	175	0	20	56	3.4
Pork fresh rib, roasted, lean + fat	3 oz.	20	270	0	21	69	7.2
Pork shoulder, braised, lean	2.4 oz.	8	165	0	22	76	2.8
Pork shoulder, braised, lean + fat	3 oz.	22	295	0	23	93	7.9
Pork, cured, bacon, reg., cooked	3 slice	9	110	0	6	16	3.3
Pork, cured, can. bacon, cooked	2 slice	4	85	1	11	27	1.3
Pork, cured, ham, canned, roast	3 oz.	7	140	0	18	35	2.4
Pork, cured, ham, roasted, lean	2.4 oz.	4	105	0	17	37	1.3
Pork, link, cooked	1 link	4	50	0	3	11	1.4
Pork, luncheon meat, canned	2 slices	13	140	1	5	26	4.5
Pork, luncheon meat, chopped ham	2 slices	7	95	0	7	21	2.4
Pork, luncheon meat, ckd. ham	2 slices	6	105	2	10	32	1.9
Potato chips	10 chips	7	105	10	1	0	1.8
Potato salad with mayonnaise	1 cup	21	360	28	7	170	3.6
Potatoes, au gratin, from mix	1 cup	10	230	31	6	12	6.3
Potatoes, baked w/o skin	1 potato	0	145	34	3	0	0
Potatoes, baked with skin	1 potato	0	220	51	5	0	.1
Potatoes, boiled	1 potato	0	115	27	2	0	0
Potatoes, hashed brown	1 cup	18	340	44	5	0	7
Potatoes, mashed, from dehydrated	1 cup	12	235	32	4	29	7.2
Potatoes, mash., rec., w/milk/mar.	1 cup	9	225	35	4	4	2.2
Potatoes, mashed, recipe, w/milk	1 cup	1	160	37	4	4	.7
Potatoes, scalloped, from mix	1 cup	11	230	31	5	27	6.5
Potatoes, French fried, frozen, fried	10	8	160	20	2	0	2.5
Potatoes, French fried, frozen, oven	10	4	110	17	2	0	2.1
Pound cake	1 slice	5	110	15	2	64	3
Pretzels, stick	10	0	10	2	0	0	0
Pretzels, twisted, Dutch	1	1	65	13	2	0	.1
Pretzels, twisted, thin	10	2	240	48	6	0	.4
Product 19 cereal	1 oz.	0	110	24	3	0	0
Provolene cheese	1 oz.	8	100	1	7	20	4.8
Prune juice, canned	1 cup	0	180	45	2	0	0
Prunes, dried	5	0	115	31	1	0	0
Prunes, dried, cooked, unsweetened	1 cup	0	225	60	2	0	0
Pudding, chocolate, canned	5 oz.	11	205	30	3	1	9.5
Pudding, choc., cooked from mix	1/2 cup	4	150	25	4	15	2.4
Pudding, choc., instant from mix	1/2 cup	4	155	27	4	14	2.3
Pudding, rice, from mix	1/2 cup	4	155	27	4	15	2.3
Pudding, tapioca, canned	5 oz.	5	160	28	3	0	4.8

Food Item	Amount	Fat Grams	Calories	Carbo Grams	Protein Grams	Chol. Mgs.	Saturated Fat
Pudding, tapioca, from mix	1/2 cup	4	145	25	4	15	2.3
Pudding, vanilla, canned	5 oz.	10	220	33	2	1	9.5
Pudding, vanilla, cooked from mix	1/2 cup	4	145	25	4	15	2.3
Pudding, vanilla, instant	1/2 cup	4	150	27	4	15	2.2
Pumpernickel bread	1 slice	1	80	16	3	0	.2
Pumpkin and squash kernels	1 oz.	13	155	5	7	0	2.5
Pumpkin pie	1 slice	17	320	37	6	109	6.4
Pumpkin, canned	1 cup	1	85	20	3	0	.4
Pumpkin, cooked	1 cup	0	50	12	2	0	.1
Quiche Lorraine	1 slice	48	600	29	13	285	23.2
Radishes, raw	4	0	5	1	0	0	0
Raisin Bran, Kellogg's	1 oz	1	90	21	3	0	.1
Raisin Bran, Post	1 oz.	1	85	21	3	0	.1
Raisin bread	1 slice	1	65	13	2	0	.2
Raisins	1 cup	1	435	115	5	0	.2
Raspberries, frozen, sweetened	1 cup	0	255	65	2	0	0
Raspberries, frozen, sweetened	10 oz.	0	295	74	2	0	0
Raspberries, raw	1 cup	1	60	14	1	0	0
Red kidney beans, dry, canned	1 cup	1	230	42	15	0	.1
Refried, beans, canned	1 cup	3	295	51	18	0	.4
Relish, sweet	1 T	0	20	5	0	0	0
Rhubarb, cooked, added sugar	1 cup	0	280	75	1	0	0
Rice Krispies cereal	1 oz.	0	110	25	2	0	0
Rice, brown, cooked	1 cup	1	230	50	5	0	.3
Rice, white, cooked	1 cup	0	225	50	4	0	.1
Rice, white, instant, cooked	1 cup	0	180	40	4	0	.1
Rice, white, parboiled, cooked	1 cup	0	185	41	4	0	0
Rice, white, parboiled, raw	1 cup	1	685	150	14	0	.1
Rice, white, raw	1 cup	1	670	149	12	0	.2
Ricotta cheese, skim milk	1 cup	19	340	13	28	76	12.1
Ricotta cheese, whole milk	1 cup	32	430	7	28	124	20.4
Roast beef sandwich	1	13	345	34	22	55	3.5
Rolls, dinner	1	2	85	14	2	0	.5
Rolls, frankfurter or hamburger	1	2	115	20	3	0	.5
Rolls, hard	1	2	155	30	5	0	.4
Rolls, hoagie or submarine	1	8	400	72	11	0	1.8
Root beer	12 F oz.	0	165	42	0	0	0
Rye bread, light	1 slice	1	65	12	2	0	.2
Rye wafers, whole-grain	2	1	55	10	1	0	.3
Safflower oil	1 cup	218	1925	0	0	0	19.8
Safflower oil	1 T	14	125	0	0	0	1.3
Salami, cooked type	2 slices	11	145	1	8	37	4.6
Salami, dry type	2 slices	7	85	1	5	16	2.4

Food Item	Amount	Fat Grams	Calories	Carbo Grams	Protein Grams	Chol. Mgs.	Saturated Fat
Salmon, baked, red	3 oz.	5	140	0	21	60	1.2
Salmon, canned, pink, w/bones	3 oz.	5	120	0	17	34	.9
Salmon, smoked	3 oz.	8	150	0	18	51	2.6
Saltines	4	1	50	9	1	4	.5
Sandwich spread, pork, beef	1 T	3	35	2	1	6	.9
Sandwich type cookie	4	8	195	29	2	0	2
Sardines, Atlantic, canned, oil, dr.	3 oz.	9	175	0	20	85	2.1
Sauerkraut, canned	1 cup	0	45	10	2	0	.1
Scallops, breaded, frozen, reheat	6	10	195	10	15	70	2.5
Seaweed, kelp, raw	1 oz.	0	10	3	0	0	.1
Seaweed, spirulina, dried	1 oz.	2	80	7	16	0	.8
Self-rising flour	1 cup	1	440	93	12	0	.2
Semisweet chocolate	1 cup	61	860	97	7	0	36.2
Sesame seeds	1 T	4	45	1	2	0	.6
Shakes, chocolate, thick	10 oz.	8	335	60	9	30	4.8
Shakes, vanilla, thick	10 oz.	9	315	50	11	33	5.3
Sheetcake, with frosting home rec.	1 piece	14	445	77	4	70	4.6
Sheetcake, w/o frosting home rec.	1 piece	12	315	48	4	61	3.3
Sherbet, 2% fat	1 cup	4	270	59	2	14	2.4
Shortbread cookie	4	8	155	20	2	27	2.9
Shredded Wheat cereal	1 oz.	1	100	23	3	0	.1
Shrimp, canned, drained	3 oz.	1	100	1	21	128	.2
Shrimp, French fried	3 oz.	10	200	11	16	168	2.5
Snack type crackers	1	1	15	2	0	0	.2
Snap bean, canned or frozen, dr.	1 cup	0	25	6	2	0	0
Snap bean, raw, cooked, drained	1 cup	0	45	10	2	0	.1
Sour cream	1 cup	48	495	10	7	102	30
Sour cream	1 T	3	25	1	0	5	1.6
Soy sauce	1 T	0	10	2	2	0	0
Soybean-cottonseed oil, hydr.	1 cup	218	1925	0	0	0	39.2
Soybean-cottonseed oil, hydr.	1 T	14	125	0	0	0	2.5
Soybean oil, hydrogenated	1 cup	218	1925	0	0	0	32.5
Soybean oil, hydrogenated	1 T	14	125	0	0	0	2.1
Soybeans, dry, cooked, drained	1 cup	10	235	19	20	0	1.3
Spaghetti, cooked, firm	1 cup	1	190	39	7	0	.1
Spaghetti, cooked, tender	1 cup	1	155	32	5	0	.1
Spaghetti, tom. sauce & cheese	1 cup	2	190	39	6	3	.4
Spaghetti and meatballs	1 cup	12	330	39	19	89	3.9
Special K Cereal	1 oz.	0	110	21	6	0	0
Spinach soufflé	1 cup	18	220	3	11	184	7.1
Spinach, canned, drained	1 cup	1	50	7	6	0	.2
Spinach, cooked	1 cup	0	40	7	5	0	.1
Spinach, raw	1 cup	0	10	2	2	0	0

Food Item	Amount	Fat Grams	Calories	Carbo Grams	Protein Grams	Chol. Mgs.	Saturated Fat
Squash, summer, cooked	1 cup	1	35	8	2	0	.1
Squash, winter, baked	1 cup	1	80	18	2	0	.3
Strawberries, frozen, sweetened	1 cup	0	245	66	1	0	0
Strawberries, frozen, sweetened	10 oz.	0	275	74	2	0	0
Strawberries, raw	1 cup	1	45	10	1	0	0
Sugar cookie, from ref. dough	4	12	235	31	2	29	2.3
Sugar Frosted Flakes, Kellogg's	1 oz.	0	110	26	1	0	0
Sugar Smacks cereal	1 oz.	1	105	25	2	0	.1
Sugar, brown	1 cup	0	820	212	0	0	0
Sugar, powdered	1	0	385	100	0	0	0
Sugar, white, granulated	1 cup	0	770	199	0	0	0
Sugar, white, granulated	1 pkt	0	25	6	0	0	0
Sugar, white, granulated	1 T	0	45	12	0	0	0
Sunflower oil	1 cup	218	1925	0	0	0	22.5
Sunflower oil	1 T	14	125	0	0	0	1.4
Sunflower seeds	1 oz.	14	160	5	6	0	1.5
Sweet (dark) chocolate	1 oz.	10	150	16	1	0	5.9
Sweetened condensed milk	1 cup	27	980	166	24	104	16.8
Sweet potatoes, baked, peeled	1	0	115	28	2	0	0
Sweet potatoes, candied	1 piece	3	145	29	1	8	1.4
Sweet potatoes, canned, mashed	1 cup	1	260	59	5	0	.1
Swiss cheese	1 oz.	8	105	1	8	26	5
Syrup, chocolate flavor, fudge	2 T	5	125	21	2	0	3.1
Table syrup (corn and maple)	2 T	0	122	32	0	0	0
Taco	1	11	195	15	9	21	4.1
Tahini	1 T	8	90	3	3	0	1.1
Tangerine juice, canned, sweet.	1 cup	0	125	30	1	0	0
Tangerines, canned, light syrup	1 cup	0	155	41	1	0	0
Tangerines, raw	1	0	35	9	1	0	0
Tartar sauce	1 T	8	75	1	0	4	1.2
Tea, brewed	8 F oz.	0	0	0	0	0	0
Tea, instant, unsweetened	8 F oz.	0	0	1	0	0	0
Tea, instant, sweetened	8 F oz.	0	85	22	0	0	0
Tofu	1 piece	5	85	3	9	0	.7
Tomato juice	1 cup	0	40	10	2	0	0
Tomato paste, canned	1 cup	2	220	49	10	0	.3
Tomato puree, canned	1 cup	0	105	25	4	0	0
Tomato sauce, canned	1 cup	0	75	18	3	0	.1
Tomato soup, w/milk, canned	1 cup	6	160	22	6	17	2.9
Tomato soup, w/water, canned	1 cup	2	85	17	2	0	.4
Tomato veg. soup, dehydrated	1 pkt.	1	40	8	1	0	.3
Tomatoes, canned	1 cup	1	50	10	2	0	.1
Tomatoes, raw	1	0	25	5	1	0	0

Food Item	Amount	Fat Grams	Calories	Carbo Grams	Protein Grams	Chol. Mgs.	Saturated Fat
Tortillas, corn	1	1	65	13	2	0	.1
Total cereal	1 oz.	1	100	22	3	0	.1
Trix cereal	1 oz.	0	110	25	2	0	.2
Trout, broiled w/butter/lemon	3 oz.	9	175	0	21	71	4.1
Tuna salad	1 cup	19	375	19	33	80	3.3
Tuna, light, can., drained, water	3 oz.	7	165	0	24	55	1.4
Tuna, white, can., drained, water	3 oz.	1	135	0	30	48	.3
Turkey, dark w/o skin	4 oz.	8.2	212	0	32.4	96	-
Turkey, light w/o skin	4 oz.	3.7	178	0	33.9	78	-
Turnip greens, cooked	1 cup	0	30	6	2	0	.1
Turnips, cooked, diced	1 cup	0	30	8	1	0	0
Vanilla wafers	10	7	185	29	2	25	1.8
Veal cutlet, medium fat	3 oz.	9	185	0	23	86	4.1
Veal rib, medium fat, roasted	3 oz.	14	230	0	23	109	6
Vegetable beef soup, canned	1 cup	2	80	10	6	5	.9
Vegetable juice cocktail, canned	1 cup	0	45	11	2	0	0
Vegetables, mixed, canned	1 cup	0	75	15	4	0	.1
Vegetables, mixed, frozen	1 cup	0	105	24	5	0	.1
Vegetarian soup	1 cup	2	70	12	2	0	.3
Vienna bread	1 slice	1	70	13	2	0	.2
Vienna sausage	1	4	45	0	2	8	1.5
Vinegar and oil salad dressing	1 T	8	70	0	0	0	1.5
Vinegar, cider	1 T	0	0	1	0	0	0
Waffles, from mix	1	8	205	27	7	59	2.7
Walnuts, black, chopped	1 cup	71	760	15	30	0	4.5
Walnuts, black, chopped	1 oz.	16	170	3	7	0	1
Water chestnuts, canned	1 cup	0	70	17	1	0	0
Watermelon, raw	1 piece	2	155	35	3	0	.3
Watermelon, raw, diced	1 cup	1	50	11	1	0	.1
Wheat bread	1 slice	1	65	12	2	0	.2
Wheat flour, all-purpose	1 cup	1	420	88	12	0	.2
Wheaties cereal	1 oz.	0	100	23	3	0	.1
Wheat, thin crackers	4	1	35	5	1	0	.5
Whipped cream, unwhipped heavy	1 cup	88	820	7	5	326	54.8
Whipped cream, unwhipped light	1 cup	74	700	7	5	265	46.2
White bread	1 slice	1	65	12	2	0	.3
White bread crumbs	1 cup	2	120	22	4	0	.6
White cake, w/frosting	1 piece	9	260	42	3	3	2.1
White sauce, w/milk from mix	1 cup	13	240	21	10	34	6.4
Whole-wheat bread	1 slice	1	70	13	3	0	.4
Whole-wheat flour	1 cup	2	400	85	16	0	.3
Whole-wheat wafer/crackers	2	2	35	5	1	0	.5
Wine cooler	12 F oz.	0	190	29	0	0	0

Food Item	Amount	Fat Grams	Calories	Carbo Grams	Protein Grams	Chol. Mgs.	Saturated Fat
Wine, dessert	3.5 F oz.	0	140	8	0	0	0
Wine, table, red	3.5 F oz.	0	75	3	0	0	0
Wine, table, white	3.5 F oz.	0	80	3	0	0	0
Yeast, baker's, dry active	1 pkg.	0	20	3	3	0	0
Yellow cake w/choc. frosting	1 piece	8	235	40	3	36	3
Yogurt, w/low-fat milk	8 oz.	4	145	16	12	14	2.3
Yogurt, w/nonfat milk	8 oz.	0	125	17	13	4	.3
Yogurt, w/whole milk	8 oz.	7	140	11	8	29	4.8

Food Item	Amount	Total Calories	Fat Calories	Total Fat (g)	Sat. Fat (g)	Chol. (mg)	Sodium (mg)	Carbo (g)	Protein (g)

Arby's®

Roast Beef Sandwiches

Food Item	Amount	Total Calories	Fat Calories	Total Fat (g)	Sat. Fat (g)	Chol. (mg)	Sodium (mg)	Carbo (g)	Protein (g)
Melt w/Cheddar	1	340	139	15	5	70	890	36	16
Arby-Q	1	360	130	14	4	70	1530	40	16
Beef 'N Cheddar	1	480	221	24	8	90	1240	43	23
Big Montana	1	630	290	32	15	155	2080	41	47
Giant Roast Beef	1	480	206	23	10	110	1440	41	32
Junior Roast Beef	1	310	121	13	4.5	70	740	34	16
Regular Roast Beef	1	350	151	16	6	85	950	34	21
Super Roast Beef	1	470	207	23	7	85	1130	47	22

Other Sandwiches

Food Item	Amount	Total Calories	Fat Calories	Total Fat (g)	Sat. Fat (g)	Chol. (mg)	Sodium (mg)	Carbo (g)	Protein (g)
Chicken Bacon 'N Swiss	1	610	293	33	8	110	1550	49	31
Chicken Breast Fillet	1	540	265	30	5	90	1160	47	24
Chicken Cordon Bleu	1	630	309	35	8	120	1820	47	34
Grilled Chicken Deluxe	1	450	198	22	4	110	1050	37	29
Roast Chicken Club	1	520	260	28	7	115	1440	38	29
Hot Ham 'N Swiss	1	340	119	13	4.5	90	1450	35	23

Sub Sandwiches

Food Item	Amount	Total Calories	Fat Calories	Total Fat (g)	Sat. Fat (g)	Chol. (mg)	Sodium (mg)	Carbo (g)	Protein (g)
French Dip	1	440	158	18	8	100	1680	42	28
Hot Ham 'N Swiss	1	530	239	27	8	110	1860	45	29
Italian	1	780	468	53	15	120	2440	49	29
Philly Beef 'N Swiss	1	700	378	42	15	130	1940	46	36
Roast Beef	1	760	426	48	16	130	2230	47	35
Turkey	1	630	328	37	9	100	2170	51	26

Market Fresh Sandwiches

Food Item	Amount	Total Calories	Fat Calories	Total Fat (g)	Sat. Fat (g)	Chol. (mg)	Sodium (mg)	Carbo (g)	Protein (g)
Roast Beef & Swiss	1	810	381	42	13	130	1780	73	37
Roast Ham & Swiss	1	730	307	34	8	125	2180	74	36
Roast Chicken Caesar	1	820	336	38	9	140	2160	75	43
Roast Turkey & Swiss	1	760	296	33	6	130	1920	75	43

Market Fresh Salads (dressing not included)

Food Item	Amount	Total Calories	Fat Calories	Total Fat (g)	Sat. Fat (g)	Chol. (mg)	Sodium (mg)	Carbo (g)	Protein (g)
Turkey Club Salad	1	350	189	21	10	90	920	9	33
Caesar Salad	1	90	34	4	2.5	10	170	8	7
Grilled Chicken Caesar	1	230	69	8	3.5	80	920	8	33
Chicken Finger Salad	1	570	308	34	9	65	1300	39	30
Caesar Side Salad	1	45	20	2	1	5	95	4	4

Food Item	Amount	Total Calories	Fat Calories	Total Fat (g)	Sat. Fat (g)	Chol. (mg)	Sodium (mg)	Carbo (g)	Protein (g)
Light Menu									
Light Grilled Chicken	1	280	48	5	1.5	55	1170	30	29
Lt Roast Chicken Deluxe	1	260	44	5	1	40	1010	33	23
Lt Roast Turkey Deluxe	1	260	44	5	0.5	40	980	33	23
Roast Chicken Salad	1	160	21	2.5	0	40	700	15	20
Grilled Chicken Salad	1	210	40	4.5	1.5	65	800	14	30
Garden Salad	1	70	5	1	0	0	45	14	4
Side Salad	1	25	0	0	0	0	20	5	2
Side Items									
Cheddar Curly Fries	1	460	221	24	6	5	1290	54	6
Curly Fries (small)	1	310	140	15	3.5	0	770	39	4
Curly Fries (medium)	1	400	180	20	5	0	990	50	5
Curly Fries (large)	1	620	273	30	7	0	1540	78	8
Homestyle Fries (child)	1	220	86	10	2.5	0	430	32	3
Homestyle Fries (small)	1	300	120	13	3.5	0	570	42	3
Homestyle Fries (med.)	1	370	141	16	4	0	710	53	4
Homestyle Fries (large)	1	560	218	24	6	0	1070	79	6
Potato Cakes	2	250	140	16	4	0	490	26	2
Jalapeno Bites	1	330	188	21	9	40	670	30	7
Mozzarella Sticks	4	470	259	29	14	60	1330	34	18
Onion Petals	1	410	221	24	3.5	0	300	43	4
Chicken Finger Snack	1	580	290	32	7	35	1450	55	19
Chicken Finger 4-Pack	1	640	352	38	8	70	1590	42	31
Baked Pot. w/Btr/Sr Crm	1	500	210	24	15	55	170	65	8
Broccoli 'N Cheddar BP	1	540	211	24	12	50	680	71	12
Deluxe Baked Potato	1	650	312	34	20	90	750	67	20
Desserts									
Iced Apple Turnover	1	420	139	16	4.5	0	230	65	4
Cherry Turnover	1	410	139	16	4.5	0	250	63	4
Breakfast Items									
Biscuit w/Butter	1	280	151	17	4	0	780	27	5
Biscuit w/Ham	1	330	182	20	5	30	830	28	12
Biscuit w/Sausage	1	460	299	33	9	25	300	28	12
Biscuit w/Bacon	1	360	220	24	7	10	220	27	9
Croissant w/Ham	1	310	171	19	11	50	1130	29	13
Croissant w/Sausage	1	440	290	32	15	45	600	29	13
Croissant w/Bacon	1	340	211	23	13	30	520	28	10
Sourdough w/Ham	1	390	47	6	1	30	1570	67	19
Sourdough w/Sausage	1	520	172	19	5	25	1040	67	19
Sourdough w/Bacon	1	420	88	10	2.5	10	960	66	16
French Toastix (no syrup)	1	370	152	17	4	0	440	48	7

Food Item	Amount	Total Calories	Fat Calories	Total Fat (g)	Sat. Fat (g)	Chol. (mg)	Sodium (mg)	Carbo (g)	Protein (g)
Condiments									
Sauce Packet	.5 oz.	15	0	0	0	0	180	4	0
BBQ Dipping Sauce	1 oz.	40	0	0	0	0	350	10	0
Au Jus Sauce	3 oz.	5	0	.05	.02	0	386	.89	.30
BBQ Vinaigrette Dressing	2 oz.	140	99	11	1.5	0	660	9	0
Bleu Cheese Dressing	2 oz.	300	279	31	6	45	580	3	2
Bronco Berry Sauce	1.5 oz.	90	0	0	0	0	35	23	0
Buttermilk Ranch Drsng.	2 oz.	360	349	39	6	5	490	2	1
Butter. Ran. Drsng. no fat	2 oz.	60	0	0	0	0	750	13	1
Caesar Dressing	2 oz.	310	310	34	5	60	470	1	1
Croutons, Cheese&Garlic	.63 oz.	100	53	6.25	n/a	n/a	138	10	2.5
Croutons, Seasoned	.25 oz.	30	10	1	0	0	70	5	1
German Mustard Packet	.25 oz.	5	0	0	0	0	60	0	0
Honey French Dressing	2 oz.	290	209	24	4	0	410	18	0
Honey Mustard Sauce	1 oz.	130	111	12	1.5	10	160	5	0
Horsey Sauce Packet	.5 oz.	60	45	5	0.5	5	150	3	0
Italian Dressing	2 oz.	25	10	1	1	0	1030	3	0
Italian Parmesan Dressing	2 oz.	240	221	24	4	0	950	4	1
Ketchup Packet	.32 oz.	10	0	0	0	0	100	2	0
French Toast Syrup	.5 oz.	130	0	0	0	0	45	32	0
Mayonnaise Packet	.44 oz.	90	90	10	1.5	10	65	0	0
Mayonnaise Packet Light	.44 oz.	20	15	1.5	0	0	110	1	0
Marinara Sauce	1.5 oz.	35	12	1	0	0	260	4	1
Tangy Southwest Sauce	1.5 oz.	250	240	26	4.5	30	290	3	0
Thousand Island Dressing	2 oz.	290	249	28	4.5	35	480	9	1
Beverages									
Milk	1	120	43	5	3	20	120	12	8
Hot Chocolate	1	110	11	1	0.5	0	120	23	2
Orange Juice	1	140	0	0	0	0	0	34	1
Vanilla Shake	1	470	141	15	7	45	360	83	10
Chocolate Shake	1	480	149	16	8	45	370	84	10
Strawberry Shake	1	500	120	13	8	15	340	87	11
Jamocha Shake	1	470	141	15	7	45	390	82	10

Burger King®

Breakfast

Food Item	Amount	Total Calories	Fat Calories	Total Fat (g)	Sat. Fat (g)	Chol. (mg)	Sodium (mg)	Carbo (g)	Protein (g)
Croissan'wich w/Egg/Ch.	1	320	170	19	7	185	730	24	12
Croissan' w/Sau../Egg/Ch.	1	520	350	39	14	210	1090	24	19
Croissan' w/Bac./Egg/Ch.	1	360	200	22	8	195	950	25	15
Croissan' w/Ham/Egg/Ch.	1	360	180	20	8	200	1500	25	18

Food Item	Amount	Total Calories	Fat Calories	Total Fat (g)	Sat. Fat (g)	Chol. (mg)	Sodium (mg)	Carbo (g)	Protein (g)
French Toast Sticks	5	390	180	20	4.5	0	440	46	7
Hash Brown Rounds	1	230	130	15	4	0	450	23	2

Burgers

Food Item	Amount	Total Calories	Fat Calories	Total Fat (g)	Sat. Fat (g)	Chol. (mg)	Sodium (mg)	Carbo (g)	Protein (g)
Whopper	1	700	370	42	13	85	1020	52	31
Whopper w/Cheese	1	800	440	49	18	110	1450	53	35
Double Whopper	1	970	550	61	23	160	1110	52	52
Double Whop. w/Cheese	1	1060	620	69	27	185	1540	53	56
Whopper Jr.	1	390	200	22	7	45	550	31	17
Whopper Jr. w/Cheese	1	430	230	26	9	55	770	32	19
Chicken Whopper	1	570	230	25	4.5	75	1410	48	38
Hamburger	1	310	120	13	5	40	550	30	17
Cheeseburger	1	350	150	17	8	50	770	31	19
Double Hamburger	1	440	210	23	10	75	600	30	28
Double Cheeseburger	1	530	280	31	15	100	1030	32	32
Bacon Cheeseburger	1	390	180	20	9	60	990	31	22
Bacon Double Cheese.	1	770	310	34	17	110	1250	31	35
Angus Steak Burger	1	570	200	22	8	180	1270	62	33
Angus Bac./Ch./St. Burger	1	710	300	33	15	215	1990	64	41
Low Carb Ang. St. Burger	1	280	160	18	7	180	730	5	25
Low Carb B.&C. St. Bur.	1	420	270	29	14	215	1450	7	33
Veggie w/Mayo	1	380	140	16	2.5	5	930	46	14

Sandwich/Side Orders

Food Item	Amount	Total Calories	Fat Calories	Total Fat (g)	Sat. Fat (g)	Chol. (mg)	Sodium (mg)	Carbo (g)	Protein (g)
Chicken Sandwich	1	560	260	28	6	60	1270	52	25
TenderCrisp Ch. Sand.	1	780	400	45	7	55	1710	70	27
Spicy T. Cr. Ch. Sand.	1	720	340	38	6	55	2030	71	27
Fish Filet Sandwich	1	710	270	30	18	55	840	44	18
Chicken Tenders	5	210	110	12	3.5	30	530	13	14
Chicken Tenders	8	340	170	19	5	50	840	20	22
Chicken Caesar Salad	1	190	60	7	3	50	900	9	25
Shrimp Caesar Salad	1	180	90	10	3	120	800	9	19
Chicken Garden Salad	1	210	60	7	3	50	910	13	26
Shrimp Garden Salad	1	200	90	10	3	120	890	12	20
Side Garden Salad	1	20	0	0	0	0	15	4	1
French Fries (small)	1	230	100	11	3	0	410	29	3
French Fries (medium)	1	360	160	18	5	0	640	46	4
French Fries (large)	1	500	220	25	7	0	880	63	6
French Fries (king)	1	600	270	30	8	0	1070	76	7
Onion Rings (small)	1	180	80	9	2	0	260	22	3
Onion Rings (medium)	1	320	140	16	4	0	460	40	4
Onion Rings (large)	1	480	210	23	6	0	690	60	7
Onion Rings (king size)	1	550	240	27	7	0	800	70	8
Chili	1	190	70	8	3	25	1040	17	13

Food Item	Amount	Total Calories	Fat Calories	Total Fat (g)	Sat. Fat (g)	Chol. (mg)	Sodium (mg)	Carbo (g)	Protein (g)
Desserts									
Dutch Apple Pie	1	340	130	14	3	3	470	52	2
Hershey's Sundae Pie	1	310	160	18	13	10	130	35	3
Vanilla Shake (small)	1	330	50	6	4	20	260	61	9
Vanilla Shake (medium)	1	430	70	8	5	25	340	79	12
Chocolate Shake (small)	1	400	50	6	4	20	360	77	10
Chocolate Shake (med.)	1	500	70	8	5	25	440	95	13
Strawberry Shake (small)	1	390	50	6	4	20	270	76	9
Strawberry Shake (med.)	1	500	70	8	5	25	350	95	12
Nestle Toll House cookies	1	440	150	16	5	20	360	68	5

Chick-fil-A®

Food Item	Amount	Total Calories	Fat Calories	Total Fat (g)	Sat. Fat (g)	Chol. (mg)	Sodium (mg)	Carbo (g)	Protein (g)
Sandwiches									
Chicken	1	410	150	16	3.5	60	1300	38	28
Chicken Deluxe	1	420	150	16	3.5	60	1300	39	28
Chargrilled Chicken	1	270	30	3.5	1	65	940	33	28
Chargrilled Chicken Club	1	380	100	11	5	90	1240	33	35
Cool Wraps									
Chargrilled Chicken	1	390	60	7	3	65	1020	54	29
Chicken Caesar	1	460	90	10	6	80	1350	52	36
Spicy Chicken	1	380	60	6	3	60	1090	52	30
Specialties									
Chick-n-strips	1	290	120	13	2.5	65	730	14	29
Nuggets	1	260	110	12	2.5	70	1090	12	26
Chicken Salad Sandwich	1	350	140	15	3	65	880	32	20
Hearty Breast of Ch. Soup	1	140	35	3.5	1	25	900	18	8
Salads									
Chargrilled Ch. Garden	1	180	60	6	3	65	620	9	22
Southwest Char. Garden	1	240	70	8	3.5	60	770	17	25
Chick-n-strips	1	390	160	18	5	80	860	22	34
Side Items									
Side Salad	1	60	25	3	1.5	10	75	4	3
Cole Slaw	1	260	280	21	3.5	25	220	17	2
Carrot & Raisin Salad	1	170	50	6	1	10	110	28	1
Waffle Potato Fries	1	280	120	14	5	15	105	37	3
Fresh Fruit Cup	1	60	0	0	0	0	0	16	1

Food Item	Amount	Total Calories	Fat Calories	Total Fat (g)	Sat. Fat (g)	Chol. (mg)	Sodium (mg)	Carbo (g)	Protein (g)
Dipping Sauces									
Polynesian	1	110	50	6	1	0	210	13	0
Barbeque	1	45	0	0	0	0	180	11	0
Honey Mustard	1	45	0	0	0	0	150	10	0
Buttermilk Ranch	1	110	110	12	2	5	200	1	0
Buffalo	1	15	15	1.5	0	0	410	1	0
Honey Roasted BBQ	1	60	50	6	1	5	90	2	0
Croutons/Kernels									
Garlic Butter Croutons	1	50	30	3	0	0	90	6	1
Hon. Roast, Sun. Ker.	1	80	60	7	1	0	38	3	2.5
Tortilla Strips	1	70	30	3.5	.5	0	53	9	2
Dressings									
Caesar	2.5	160	150	17	2.5	30	240	1	1
Red. Fat Rasp. Vinaigrette	2	80	20	2	0	0	190	15	0
Blue Cheese	2.5	150	140	16	3	20	300	1	1
Buttermilk Ranch	2.5	160	150	16	2.5	5	270	1	0
Spicy	2.5	140	130	14	2	5	130	2	0
Thousand Island	2.5	150	130	14	2	10	250	5	0
Light Italian	2	15	5	.5	0	0	570	2	0
Fat Free Honey Mustard	2	60	0	0	0	0	200	14	0
Desserts									
Icedream Cup	1	230	50	6	3.5	25	100	38	5
Icedream Cone	1	160	35	4	2	15	80	28	4
Lemon Pie	1	320	90	10	3.5	110	220	51	7
Fudge Nut Brownie	1	330	140	15	3.5	20	210	45	4
Cheesecake	1	340	190	21	12	90	270	30	6
Breakfast Ingredients									
Plain Biscuit	1	260	90	11	2.5	0	670	38	4
Hot Buttered Biscuit	1	270	110	12	3	0	680	38	4
Chicken Biscuit	1	400	160	18	4.5	30	1200	43	16
Ch. Biscuit with Cheese	1	450	200	23	7	45	1430	43	19
Biscuit with Bacon	1	300	130	14	4	5	780	38	6
Biscuit w/Bacon and Egg	1	390	180	20	6	250	860	38	13
Bis. w/Bacon, Egg, & Ch.	1	430	220	24	9	265	1070	38	16
Biscuit with Egg	1	340	150	16	4.5	245	740	38	11
Biscuit with Egg & Ch.	1	390	190	21	7	260	960	38	13
Biscuit with Sausage	1	410	210	23	9	20	740	42	9
Biscuit with Saus. & Egg	1	500	260	29	11	265	810	43	15
Biscuit w/Saus./Egg/Ch.	1	540	300	33	13	280	1030	43	18
Biscuit with Gravy	1	310	120	13	3.5	5	930	44	5

Food Item	Amount	Total Calories	Fat Calories	Total Fat (g)	Sat. Fat (g)	Chol. (mg)	Sodium (mg)	Carbo (g)	Protein (g)
Hashbrowns	1	170	80	9	4.5	10	350	20	2
Danish	1	430	150	17	4.5	25	160	63	6

Dairy Queen®

Burgers
Homestyle Hamburger	1	290	110	12	5	45	630	29	17
Homestyle Cheeseburger	1	340	150	17	8	55	850	29	20
Home. Double Cheese.	1	540	280	31	16	115	1130	30	35
Home. Bac. Dble. Cheese.	1	610	320	36	18	130	1380	31	41
Ultimate Burger	1	670	390	43	19	135	1210	29	40

Hot Dogs
Hot Dog	1	240	120	14	5	25	730	19	9
Chili 'n' Cheese Dog	1	330	190	21	9	45	1090	22	14

Sandwiches/Baskets
Breaded Chicken Sand.	1	510	240	27	4	40	1070	47	19
Grilled Chick. Sandwich	1	340	150	16	2.5	50	1000	26	22
Chicken Strip Basket	1	1000	450	50	13	55	2510	102	35

Fries/Onion Rings
French Fries (small)	1	300	110	12	2.5	0	700	45	3
French Fries (medium)	1	380	140	15	3	0	880	56	4
French Fries (large)	1	480	170	19	4	0	1140	72	5
Onion Rings	1	470	270	30	6	0	740	45	6

Salads
Crispy Chicken (no dress.)	1	350	180	20	6	40	620	21	21
Grilled Chick. (no dress.)	1	240	90	10	5	65	950	12	26
Side Salad	1	60	25	2.5	1.5	5	60	6	3

Salad Dressings
Honey Mustard	1	260	190	21	3.5	20	370	18	1
Wish-bone Fat Free Ital.	1	25	0	0	0	0	520	6	0
Blue Cheese	1	210	180	20	4	5	700	4	2
Ranch	1	310	300	33	5	25	390	3	1
Fat Free Honey Mustard	1	50	0	0	0	0	160	13	0
Red. Cal. Buttermilk	1	140	120	13	2	15	390	5	0
Fat Free Thousand Island	1	60	0	0	0	0	400	16	0
Fat Free Ranch	1	60	0	0	0	0	410	13	1
Fat Free Red French	1	40	0	0	0	0	330	10	0
Fat Free Italian	1	10	0	0	0	0	390	3	0
Fat Free Buttermilk Ran.	1	30	0	0	0	0	440	6	1

Food Item	Amount	Total Calories	Fat Calories	Total Fat (g)	Sat. Fat (g)	Chol. (mg)	Sodium (mg)	Carbo (g)	Protein (g)
Cones									
Vanilla Soft Serve	1/2 cup	140	40	4.5	3	15	70	22	3
Chocolate Soft Serve	1/2 cup	150	45	5	3.5	15	75	22	4
Small Vanilla	1	230	60	7	4.5	20	115	38	6
Medium Vanilla	1	330	90	9	6	30	160	53	8
Large Vanilla	1	480	130	15	9	45	230	76	11
Small Chocolate	1	240	70	8	5	20	115	37	6
Medium Chocolate	1	340	100	11	7	30	160	53	8
Small Dipped	1	340	150	17	9	20	130	42	6
Medium Dipped	1	490	220	24	13	30	190	59	8
Large Dipped	1	710	330	36	17	45	250	85	12
Malts, Shakes, and Misty									
Small Choc. Malt	1	640	150	16	11	55	340	111	15
Medium Choc. Malt	1	870	200	22	14	70	450	153	20
Large Choc. Malt	1	1320	310	35	22	110	670	222	29
Small Choc. Shake	1	560	140	15	10	50	280	93	13
Medium Choc. Shake	1	760	180	20	12	70	370	129	17
Large Choc. Shake	1	1140	300	33	21	105	550	186	26
Small Misty Slush	1	220	0	0	0	0	20	56	0
Medium Misty Slush	1	290	0	0	0	0	30	74	0
Sundaes									
Small Strawberry	1	240	60	7	4.5	20	110	40	5
Medium Strawberry	1	340	80	9	6	30	160	58	7
Large Strawberry	1	500	130	15	9	45	230	83	10
Small Chocolate	1	280	60	7	4.5	20	140	49	5
Medium Chocolate	1	400	90	10	6	30	210	71	8
Large Chocolate	1	580	140	15	10	45	260	100	11
Royal Treats									
Banana Split	1	510	100	12	8	30	180	96	8
Peanut Buster Parfait	1	730	280	31	17	35	400	99	16
Pecan Praline Parfait	1	720	260	29	11	30	610	105	9
Triple Chocolate Utopia	1	770	350	39	17	55	390	96	12
Strawberry Shortcake	1	430	120	14	9	60	360	70	7
Brownie Earthquake	1	740	240	27	16	50	350	112	10
Novelties									
DQ Sandwich	1	220	60	6	3	10	140	31	4
Chocolate Dilly Bar	1	210	120	13	7	10	75	21	3
Buster Bar	1	450	260	28	12	15	280	41	10
Starkiss	1	80	0	0	0	0	10	21	0
Fudge Bar	1	50	0	0	0	0	70	13	4

Food Item	Amount	Total Calories	Fat Calories	Total Fat (g)	Sat. Fat (g)	Chol. (mg)	Sodium (mg)	Carbo (g)	Protein (g)
Vanilla Orange Bar	1	60	0	0	0	0	40	17	2
Lemon DQ Freez'r	1/2 cup	80	0	0	0	0	10	20	0

Blizzard Treats

Food Item	Amount	Total Calories	Fat Calories	Total Fat (g)	Sat. Fat (g)	Chol. (mg)	Sodium (mg)	Carbo (g)	Protein (g)
Small Oreo Cookies	1	570	190	21	10	40	430	83	11
Medium Oreo Cookies	1	700	240	26	12	45	560	103	13
Large Oreo Cookies	1	1010	340	37	18	70	770	148	19
Small Choc. Chip Ck. D.	1	720	250	28	14	50	370	105	12
Med. Choc. Chip Ck. D.	1	1030	360	40	20	70	520	150	17
Large Choc. Chip Ck. D.	1	1320	470	52	26	90	670	193	21
Small Banana Split	1	460	130	14	9	40	210	73	10
Medium Banana Split	1	580	150	17	11	50	260	97	12
Large Banana Split	1	810	210	23	15	70	360	134	17

Domino's Pizza®

12" Cheese

Food Item	Amount	Total Calories	Fat Calories	Total Fat (g)	Sat. Fat (g)	Chol. (mg)	Sodium (mg)	Carbo (g)	Protein (g)
Hand-Tossed	1/8	186	-	5.5	2	9	385	28	7
Deep Dish	1/8	238	-	11	3.5	11	555	28	9
Crunch Thin	1/8	137	-	7	2.5	10	292	14	5

12" Pepperoni

Food Item	Amount	Total Calories	Fat Calories	Total Fat (g)	Sat. Fat (g)	Chol. (mg)	Sodium (mg)	Carbo (g)	Protein (g)
Hand-Tossed	1/8	223	-	9	3.5	16	521	28	9
Deep Dish	1/8	275	-	14	5	19	692	14	5
Crunch Thin	1/8	174	-	10	4	17	429	14	7

12" Sausage

Food Item	Amount	Total Calories	Fat Calories	Total Fat (g)	Sat. Fat (g)	Chol. (mg)	Sodium (mg)	Carbo (g)	Protein (g)
Hand-Tossed	1/8	231	-	9.5	3.5	17	530	28	9
Deep Dish	1/8	283	-	15	5	19	701	29	11
Crunch Thin	1/8	206	-	13.5	5	23	533	14	8

12" Pepperoni & Sausage

Food Item	Amount	Total Calories	Fat Calories	Total Fat (g)	Sat. Fat (g)	Chol. (mg)	Sodium (mg)	Carbo (g)	Protein (g)
Hand-Tossed	1/8	255	-	11.5	4.5	22	625	28	10
Deep Dish	1/8	307	-	17	6	25	796	29	12
Crunch Thin	1/8	206	-	13.5	5	23	533	14	8

12" Ham & Pineapple

Food Item	Amount	Total Calories	Fat Calories	Total Fat (g)	Sat. Fat (g)	Chol. (mg)	Sodium (mg)	Carbo (g)	Protein (g)
Hand-Tossed	1/8	200	-	6	2.5	12	466	29	9
Deep Dish	1/8	252	-	1.5	4	15	637	30	10
Crunch Thin	1/8	150	-	7.5	3	13	374	15	7

12" Ham

Food Item	Amount	Total Calories	Fat Calories	Total Fat (g)	Sat. Fat (g)	Chol. (mg)	Sodium (mg)	Carbo (g)	Protein (g)
Hand-Tossed	1/8	198	-	6	2.5	13	492	28	9
Deep Dish	1/8	250	-	11.5	4	16	663	28	11
Crunch Thin	1/8	148	-	7.5	3	14	399	14	7

12" Green Pepper, Onion, & Mushroom

Food Item	Amount	Total Calories	Fat Calories	Total Fat (g)	Sat. Fat (g)	Chol. (mg)	Sodium (mg)	Carbo (g)	Protein (g)
Hand-Tossed	1/8	191	-	5.5	2	9	385	29	8

Food Item	Amount	Total Calories	Fat Calories	Total Fat (g)	Sat. Fat (g)	Chol. (mg)	Sodium (mg)	Carbo (g)	Protein (g)
Deep Dish	1/8	244	-	11	3.5	11	556	30	9
Crunch Thin	1/8	142	-	7.5	2.5	10	293	15	6
12" Beef									
Hand-Tossed	1/8	225	-	9	3.5	16	493	28	9
Deep Dish	1/8	277	-	14.5	5	19	663	28	11
Crunch Thin	1/8	175	-	10.5	4	17	400	14	7
Side Dishes									
Buffalo Chicken Kickers	1	47	-	2	.5	9	162	3	4
Hot Buffalo Wings	1	45	-	2.5	.5	26	254	3	5
BBQ Buffalo Wings	1	50	-	2.5	.5	26	175	2	6
Hot Dipping Sauce	1	15	-	0	0	0	1820	4	0
Blue Cheese Dipping Sauce	1	223	-	23.5	4	20	417	2	1
Ranch Dipping Sauce	1	197	-	20.5	3	9	380	2	1
Breadsticks	1	115	-	6.3	1.1	0	122	12	2
Cheesy Bread	1	123	-	6.5	1.9	6	162	13	4
Marinara Dipping Sauce	1	25	-	.2	0	0	262	5	1
Garlic Sauce	1	440	-	49	10	0	380	0	0
Cinna Stix	1	123	-	6	1	0	111	15	2
Sweet Icing	1	250	-	2.5	2.5	0	0	57	0

Kentucky Fried Chicken®

Chicken

Food Item	Amount	Total Calories	Fat Calories	Total Fat (g)	Sat. Fat (g)	Chol. (mg)	Sodium (mg)	Carbo (g)	Protein (g)
Original Recipe									
Whole Wing	1	150	90	9	2.5	60	370	5	11
Chicken Breast	1	380	220	19	6	145	1150	11	40
Drumstick	1	140	80	8	2	75	440	4	4
Thigh	1	360	160	25	7	165	1060	12	22
Extra Crispy									
Whole Wing	1	180	140	12	4	55	390	10	10
Breast	1	460	240	28	8	160	874	17	39
Drumstick	1	160	110	10	2.5	70	420	5	12
Thigh	1	370	250	26	7	120	710	12	21
Hot & Spicy									
Whole Wing	1	180	130	11	8	60	420	9	11
Breast	1	460	270	27	8	130	1450	20	33
Drumstick	1	150	90	9	2.5	65	380	4	13
Thigh	1	400	225	28	8	125	1240	14	22

Food Item	Amount	Total Calories	Fat Calories	Total Fat (g)	Sat. Fat (g)	Chol. (mg)	Sodium (mg)	Carbo (g)	Protein (g)
Sandwiches									
Original Recipe									
w/Sauce	1	450	240	27	6	65	1010	22	29
no sauce	1	320	120	13	4	60	890	21	29
Triple Crunch									
w/Sauce	1	670	360	40	8	80	1640	42	36
no sauce	1	540	230	26	6	75	1510	41	35
Triple Crunch Zinger									
w/Sauce	1	680	370	41	8	90	1650	42	35
no sauce	1	540	230	26	6	75	1510	41	35
Tender Roast									
w/Sauce	1	390	170	19	4	70	810	24	31
no sauce	1	260	45	5	1.5	65	690	23	31
Honey BBQ Flavored	1	300	50	6	1.5	150	640	41	21
Twister	1	670	300	38	7	60	1650	55	27
Crispy Strips									
Colonel's Crispy Strips	3	400	125	24	5	75	1250	17	29
Popcorn Chicken									
Small	1	450	270	29	6	50	1030	26	19
Large	1	650	400	43	10	70	1530	38	29
Pot Pie									
Chunky Chicken	1	770	378	40	15	115	1680	70	33
Wings									
Hot Wings Pieces	6	450	297	29	6	145	1120	23	24
Honey BBQ Wings	6	540	300	33	7	-	1130	36	15
Vegetables									
Mashed Potatoes w/Gravy	1	120	40	4.5	1	0	380	18	2
Potato Wedges	1	240	110	12	3	0	830	30	5
Macaroni & Cheese	1	130	50	6	2	5	610	15	5
Corn on the Cob	1	150	25	3	1	0	10	26	5
BBQ Baked Beans	1	230	10	1	1	0	720	46	8
Cole Slaw	1	190	100	11	2	5	300	22	1
Potato Salad	1	150	80	9	1.5	5	470	22	2
Green Beans	1	50	10	1.5	0	5	570	7	2
Breads									
Biscuit	1	190	90	10	2	1.5	580	23	2
Desserts									
Chocolate Chip Cake	1	320	140	16	4	55	230	41	4

Food Item	Amount	Total Calories	Fat Calories	Total Fat (g)	Sat. Fat (g)	Chol. (mg)	Sodium (mg)	Carbo (g)	Protein (g)
Fudge Brownie Parfait	1	280	90	10	3.5	145	190	44	3
Lemon Creme Parfait	1	410	130	14	8	20	290	62	7
Chocolate Creme Parfait	1	290	130	15	11	15	330	37	3
Straw. Shortcake Parfait	1	200	60	7	6	10	220	33	1
Pecan Pie Slice	1	490	200	23	5	65	510	66	5
Apple Pie Slice	1	310	130	14	3	0	280	44	2
Straw. Creme Pie Slice	1	280	130	15	8	15	130	32	4

McDonald's®

Sandwiches

Food Item	Amount	Total Calories	Fat Calories	Total Fat (g)	Sat. Fat (g)	Chol. (mg)	Sodium (mg)	Carbo (g)	Protein (g)
Hamburger	1	280	90	10	4	30	550	36	12
Cheeseburger	1	330	130	14	6	45	790	36	15
Double Cheeseburger	1	490	240	26	12	85	1220	38	25
Quarter Pounder	1	430	190	21	8	70	770	38	23
Quar. Pounder w/Cheese	1	540	260	29	13	95	1240	39	29
D. Quar. Pound. w/Cheese	1	770	430	47	20	165	1440	39	46
Big Mac	1	600	300	33	11	85	1050	50	8
Big N' Tasty	1	540	290	32	10	80	780	38	9
Big N' Tasty w/Cheese	1	590	330	36	12	95	1020	39	9
Filet-O-Fish	1	410	180	20	4	45	660	41	15
Chicken McGrill	1	400	140	16	3	70	1020	37	27
Crispy Chicken	1	510	230	26	4.5	50	1090	47	22
McChicken®	1	430	200	23	4.5	45	830	41	14
Hot 'n Spicy McChicken	1	450	230	26	5	45	820	40	15

French Fries

Food Item	Amount	Total Calories	Fat Calories	Total Fat (g)	Sat. Fat (g)	Chol. (mg)	Sodium (mg)	Carbo (g)	Protein (g)
Small	1	220	100	11	2	0	150	28	3
Medium	1	350	150	17	3	0	220	44	5
Large	1	520	230	25	4.5	0	340	66	7
Ketchup Packet	1	10	0	0	0	0	115	3	0
Salt Packet	1	0	0	0	0	0	270	0	0

Chicken McNuggets

Food Item	Amount	Total Calories	Fat Calories	Total Fat (g)	Sat. Fat (g)	Chol. (mg)	Sodium (mg)	Carbo (g)	Protein (g)
Chicken McNuggets	4	170	90	10	2	25	450	10	10
Chicken McNuggets	6	250	130	15	3	35	670	15	15
Chicken McNuggets	10	420	220	24	5	60	1120	26	25
Chicken McNuggets	20	840	440	49	11	125	2240	51	50
Barbeque Sauce	1	45	0	0	0	0	250	10	0
Honey	1	45	0	0	0	0	0	12	0
Hot Mustard Sauce	1	60	30	3.5	0	5	240	7	1
Sweet 'N Sour Sauce	1	50	0	0	0	0	140	11	0

Food Item	Amount	Total Calories	Fat Calories	Total Fat (g)	Sat. Fat (g)	Chol. (mg)	Sodium (mg)	Carbo (g)	Protein (g)
Chicken Selects Premium Breast Strips									
Premium Breast Strips	3	380	170	19	3	50	960	28	23
Premium Breast Strips	5	630	290	32	5	85	1590	47	38
Premium Breast Strips	10	1250	570	64	10	170	3180	94	76
Spicy Buffalo Sauce	1	60	60	7	1	0	430	2	0
Creamy Ranch Sauce	1	210	200	22	3.5	10	310	2	0
Tangy Honey Mustard Sauce	1	70	25	2.5	0	10	170	12	1
Salads									
Gr. Chick./Bacon/Ranch	1	250	90	10	4.5	85	930	9	31
Cr. Chick./Bacon Ranch	1	350	180	19	6	65	1000	20	26
Bacon Ranch	1	130	70	8	4	25	280	7	10
Grilled Chicken Caesar	1	200	50	6	3	70	820	9	29
Crispy Chicken Caesar	1	310	140	16	4.5	50	890	20	23
Caesar	1	90	35	4	2.5	10	170	7	7
Gr. Ch. California Cobb	1	270	100	11	5	145	1060	9	33
Cr. Ch. California Cobb	1	370	190	21	6	125	1130	20	27
California Cobb w/o Ch.	1	150	80	9	4.5	85	410	7	11
Side	1	15	0	0	0	0	10	3	1
Butter Garlic Croutons	1	50	15	1.5	0	0	140	8	1
Fiesta w/Sour Cr./Salsa	1	450	250	27	13	95	920	28	24
Fiesta with Salsa	1	390	200	22	10	80	870	26	23
Fiesta with Sour Cream	1	420	240	27	13	95	630	21	22
Fiesta	1	360	200	22	10	80	580	19	21
Salad Dressings									
Newman's Own Cobb	2 F oz.	120	80	9	1.5	10	440	9	1
New. Own Cr. Caesar	2 F oz.	190	170	18	3.5	20	500	4	2
N. O. Low Fat Bal. Vin.	1.5 F oz.	40	25	3	0	0	730	4	0
Newman's Own Ranch	2 F oz.	170	130	15	2.5	20	530	9	1
Newman's Own Salsa	3 F oz.	30	0	0	0	0	290	7	1
Breakfast									
Egg McMuffin	1	300	110	12	5	235	850	28	18
Sausage McMuffin	1	370	200	23	9	50	790	28	14
Sausage McMuffin w/Egg	1	450	250	28	10	260	940	29	20
English Muffin	1	150	15	2	0.5	0	260	27	5
Bacon/Egg/Cheese Bis.	1	430	230	26	8	240	1230	31	18
Sausage Biscuit with Egg	1	490	300	33	10	245	1010	31	16
Sausage Biscuit	1	410	250	28	8	35	930	30	10
Biscuit	1	240	100	11	2.5	0	640	30	4
McGriddles Bacon/Egg/Ch.	1	440	190	21	7	240	1270	43	19

Food Item	Amount	Total Calories	Fat Calories	Total Fat (g)	Sat. Fat (g)	Chol. (mg)	Sodium (mg)	Carbo (g)	Protein (g)
Saus./Egg/Ch.	1	550	300	33	11	260	1290	43	20
Sausage	1	420	210	23	7	35	970	42	11
Ham/Egg/Cheese Bagel	1	550	200	23	8	255	1500	58	26
Spanish Omelet Bagel	1	710	360	40	15	275	1520	59	27
Steak/Egg/Cheese Bagel	1	640	280	31	12	265	1540	57	31
Bagel (plain)	1	260	10	1	0	0	520	54	9
Big Breakfast	1	700	420	47	13	455	1430	45	24
Deluxe Breakfast	1	1190	550	61	15	470	1990	130	30
Sausage Burrito	1	290	150	16	6	170	680	24	13
Hotcakes and Sausage	1	780	300	33	9	50	1060	104	15
Hotcakes (marg. & syrup)	1	600	150	17	3	20	770	104	9
Sausage	1	170	150	16	5	35	290	0	6
Scrambled Eggs	2	160	100	11	3.5	425	170	1	13
Hash Browns	1	130	70	8	1.5	0	330	14	1
Warm Cinnamon Roll	1	440	170	19	5	80	330	60	7
Del. Warm Cin. Roll	1	510	210	23	8	60	660	81	8
Grape Jam	.5 oz.	35	0	0	0	0	0	9	0
Strawberry Preserves	.5 oz.	35	0	0	0	0	0	9	0

Desserts/Shakes

Food Item	Amount	Total Calories	Fat Calories	Total Fat (g)	Sat. Fat (g)	Chol. (mg)	Sodium (mg)	Carbo (g)	Protein (g)
Fruit 'n Yogurt Parfait	1	160	20	2	1	5	85	30	4
F. 'n Y. Par. w/o granola	1	130	15	2	1	5	55	25	4
Apple Dippers	1	35	0	0	0	0	0	8	0
Ap. Dip. w/Low Fat Car.	1	100	5	1	0.5	5	35	22	0
Low Fat Caramel Dip	.8 oz.	70	5	1	0.5	5	35	14	0
Van. Rd. Fat Ice Cr. Cone	1	150	40	4.5	3	20	75	23	4
Kiddie Cone	1	45	15	1.5	1	5	20	7	1
Strawberry Sundae	1	290	70	7	5	30	95	50	7
Hot Caramel Sundae	1	360	90	10	6	35	180	61	7
Hot Fudge Sundae	1	340	100	12	9	30	170	52	8
Nuts (for Sundaes)	.3 oz.	40	30	3.5	0	0	55	2	2
M&M McFlurry	1	630	200	23	15	75	210	90	16
Oreo McFlurry	1	570	180	20	12	70	280	82	15
Choc. Triple Thick Shake	12 F oz.	430	110	12	8	50	210	70	11
Choc. Triple Thick Shake	16 F oz.	580	150	17	11	65	280	94	15
Choc. Triple Thick Shake	21 F oz.	750	200	22	14	90	360	123	19
Choc. Triple Thick Shake	32 F oz.	1150	300	33	22	135	550	187	30
Straw. Triple Thick Shake	12 F oz.	420	110	12	8	50	140	67	11
Straw. Triple Thick Shake	16 F oz.	560	150	16	11	65	190	89	14
Straw. Triple Thick Shake	21 F oz.	730	190	21	14	90	250	116	19
Straw. Triple Thick Shake	32 F oz.	1120	290	32	22	135	380	178	28
Van. Triple Thick Shake	12 F oz.	430	110	12	8	50	300	67	11
Van. Triple Thick Shake	16 F oz.	570	150	16	11	65	400	89	14

Food Item	Amount	Total Calories	Fat Calories	Total Fat (g)	Sat. Fat (g)	Chol. (mg)	Sodium (mg)	Carbo (g)	Protein (g)
Van. Triple Thick Shake	21 F oz.	750	190	21	14	90	530	116	18
Van. Triple Thick Shake	32 F oz.	1140	290	32	22	135	810	178	28
Baked Apple Pie	1	260	120	13	3.5	0	200	34	3
Mc. Choc. Chip Cookies	2 oz.	280	130	14	8	40	170	37	3
Mc. Cookies	2 oz.	230	70	8	2	0	250	38	3
Chocolate Chip Cookie	1	160	70	8	2	5	125	22	2
Oatmeal Raisin Cookie	1	150	50	6	1	5	100	23	2
Sugar Cookie	1	140	60	6	1	10	120	20	2

Pizza Hut®

12" Medium Pan Pizza

Food Item	Amount	Total Calories	Fat Calories	Total Fat (g)	Sat. Fat (g)	Chol. (mg)	Sodium (mg)	Carbo (g)	Protein (g)
Cheese Only	1 piece	280	120	13	5	25	500	29	11
Pepperoni	1 piece	290	130	15	5	25	560	29	11
Quartered Ham	1 piece	260	100	11	4	20	540	29	11
Supreme	1 piece	320	150	16	6	25	650	30	13
Super Supreme	1 piece	340	160	18	6	35	760	30	14
Chicken Supreme	1 piece	280	100	12	4	25	530	30	13
Meat Lover's	1 piece	340	170	19	7	35	750	29	15
Veggie Lover's	1 piece	260	100	12	4	15	470	30	10
Pepperoni Lover's	1 piece	340	170	19	7	40	700	29	15
Sausage Lover's	1 piece	330	160	17	6	30	640	29	13

12" Medium Thin 'N Crispy Pizza

Food Item	Amount	Total Calories	Fat Calories	Total Fat (g)	Sat. Fat (g)	Chol. (mg)	Sodium (mg)	Carbo (g)	Protein (g)
Cheese Only	1 piece	200	80	8	4.5	25	490	21	10
Pepperoni	1 piece	210	90	10	4.5	25	550	21	10
Quartered Ham	1 piece	180	60	6	3	20	530	21	10
Supreme	1 piece	240	100	11	5	25	640	22	11
Super Supreme	1 piece	260	120	13	6	35	760	23	13
Chicken Supreme	1 piece	200	60	7	3.5	25	520	22	12
Meat Lover's	1 piece	270	130	14	6	35	740	21	13
Veggie Lover's	1 piece	180	60	7	3	15	480	23	8
Pepperoni Lover's	1 piece	260	120	14	7	40	690	21	13
Sausage Lover's	1 piece	240	110	13	6	30	630	21	11

12" Medium Hand-Tossed Pizza

Food Item	Amount	Total Calories	Fat Calories	Total Fat (g)	Sat. Fat (g)	Chol. (mg)	Sodium (mg)	Carbo (g)	Protein (g)
Cheese Only	1 piece	240	70	8	4.5	25	520	30	12
Pepperoni	1 piece	250	80	9	4.5	25	570	29	12
Quartered Ham	1 piece	220	50	6	3	20	550	29	12
Supreme	1 piece	270	100	11	5	25	660	30	12
Super Supreme	1 piece	300	110	13	6	35	780	31	15
Chicken Supreme	1 piece	230	60	6	3	25	550	30	14
Meat Lover's	1 piece	300	120	13	6	35	760	29	15

Food Item	Amount	Total Calories	Fat Calories	Total Fat (g)	Sat. Fat (g)	Chol. (mg)	Sodium (mg)	Carbo (g)	Protein (g)
Veggie Lover's	1 piece	220	60	6	3	15	490	31	10
Pepperoni Lover's	1 piece	300	120	13	7	40	710	30	15
Sausage Lover's	1 piece	280	110	12	5	30	650	30	13

14" Stuffed Crust Pizza

Food Item	Amount	Total Calories	Fat Calories	Total Fat (g)	Sat. Fat (g)	Chol. (mg)	Sodium (mg)	Carbo (g)	Protein (g)
Cheese Only	1 piece	360	120	13	8	40	920	43	18
Pepperoni	1 piece	370	130	15	8	45	970	42	18
Quartered Ham	1 piece	340	100	11	6	40	960	42	18
Supreme	1 piece	400	150	16	8	45	1070	44	20
Super Supreme	1 piece	440	180	20	9	50	1270	45	21
Chicken Supreme	1 piece	380	120	13	7	40	1020	44	20
Meat Lover's	1 piece	450	190	21	10	55	1120	43	21
Veggie Lover's	1 piece	360	120	14	7	335	980	45	16
Pepperoni Lover's	1 piece	420	170	19	10	55	1120	43	21
Sausage Lover's	1 piece	430	170	13	9	50	1130	43	19

16" Extra Large Pizza

Food Item	Amount	Total Calories	Fat Calories	Total Fat (g)	Sat. Fat (g)	Chol. (mg)	Sodium (mg)	Carbo (g)	Protein (g)
Cheese Only	1 piece	420	140	15	8	45	1080	51	20
Pepperoni	1 piece	430	150	17	8	45	1130	50	19
Quartered Ham	1 piece	380	100	12	6	45	1110	50	19
Supreme	1 piece	460	170	19	9	45	1250	53	22
Super Supreme	1 piece	490	190	21	9	55	1430	53	23
Chicken Supreme	1 piece	400	110	12	6	40	1070	52	22
Meat Lover's	1 piece	500	200	22	10	60	1400	51	24
Veggie Lover's	1 piece	390	110	12	6	30	1030	53	17
Pepperoni Lover's	1 piece	520	210	24	11	65	1370	51	25
Sausage Lover's	1 piece	510	210	23	10	55	1330	51	23

6" Personal Pan Pizza

Food Item	Amount	Total Calories	Fat Calories	Total Fat (g)	Sat. Fat (g)	Chol. (mg)	Sodium (mg)	Carbo (g)	Protein (g)
Cheese Only	1 piece	160	60	7	3	15	310	18	7
Pepperoni	1 piece	170	70	8	3	15	340	18	7
Quartered Ham	1 piece	150	50	6	2	15	330	18	7
Supreme	1 piece	190	80	9	3.5	20	420	19	8
Super Supreme	1 piece	200	90	10	4	20	480	19	9
Chicken Supreme	1 piece	160	50	6	2.5	15	320	19	8
Meat Lover's	1 piece	200	90	10	4	20	470	18	9
Veggie Lover's	1 piece	150	50	6	2	10	280	19	6
Pepperoni Lover's	1 piece	200	90	10	4.5	25	440	18	9
Sausage Lover's	1 piece	190	90	10	4	20	400	18	8

Fit 'N Delicious 12" Medium

Food Item	Amount	Total Calories	Fat Calories	Total Fat (g)	Sat. Fat (g)	Chol. (mg)	Sodium (mg)	Carbo (g)	Protein (g)
Diced Ch./R. On./Gr. Pep.	1 piece	170	40	4.5	2	15	460	23	10
Diced Ch./Mush./Jalapeno	1 piece	170	45	5	2	15	690	22	10
Ham/Red Onion/Mush.	1 piece	160	40	4.5	2	15	470	24	8

Food Item	Amount	Total Calories	Fat Calories	Total Fat (g)	Sat. Fat (g)	Chol. (mg)	Sodium (mg)	Carbo (g)	Protein (g)
Ham/Pine./D. Red Tomato	1 piece	160	35	4	2	15	470	24	8
Gr.Pep./R. On./D. R. Tom.	1 piece	150	35	4	2	15	470	24	6
Tom./Mushroom/Jalapeno	1 piece	150	40	4	2	10	590	22	6

P'Zone

Food Item	Amount	Total Calories	Fat Calories	Total Fat (g)	Sat. Fat (g)	Chol. (mg)	Sodium (mg)	Carbo (g)	Protein (g)
Pepperoni	1	610	200	22	11	55	1280	69	34
Classic	1	610	190	21	11	50	1210	71	33
Meat Lover's	1	680	250	28	14	65	1540	70	38
Marinara Dippling Sauce	1	45	0	0	0	0	380	9	2

Appetizers

Food Item	Amount	Total Calories	Fat Calories	Total Fat (g)	Sat. Fat (g)	Chol. (mg)	Sodium (mg)	Carbo (g)	Protein (g)
Hot Wings	2	110	60	6	2	70	450	1	11
Mild Wings	2	110	60	7	2	70	320	1	11
Wing Ranch Dip. Sauce	1.5 oz.	210	200	22	3.5	10	340	4	1
Wing Blue Cheese D. S.	1.5 oz.	230	210	24	5	25	550	2	2
Breadsticks	1	150	60	6	1	0	220	20	4
Cheese Breadsticks	1	200	90	10	3.5	15	340	21	7
Breadstick Dip. Sauce	3 oz.	50	0	0	0	0	370	11	1

Desserts

Food Item	Amount	Total Calories	Fat Calories	Total Fat (g)	Sat. Fat (g)	Chol. (mg)	Sodium (mg)	Carbo (g)	Protein (g)
Cinnamon Sticks	2	170	45	5	1	0	170	27	4
White Icing Dipping Cup	2 oz.	190	0	0	0	0	0	46	0
Apple Dessert Pizza	1	260	30	3.5	.5	0	250	53	4
Cherry Dessert Pizza	1	240	30	3.5	.5	0	250	47	4

Subway®

6" Sandwiches with 6 grams of fat or less

Food Item	Amount	Total Calories	Fat Calories	Total Fat (g)	Sat. Fat (g)	Chol. (mg)	Sodium (mg)	Carbo (g)	Protein (g)
Ham	1	290	45	5	1.5	25	1270	46	18
Honey Mustard Ham	1	310	45	5	2	25	1410	54	19
Oven Roasted Ch. Br.	1	236	330	50	2	45	1010	47	24
Roast Beef	1	290	45	5	2	20	910	45	19
Savory Turkey Breast	1	280	40	4	2	20	1010	46	18
Sav.Turkey Br. & Ham	1	290	45	5	2	25	1220	47	20
Sweet Onion Ch. Teriyaki	1	370	45	5	2	50	1100	58	26
Tur. Br./Ham/Roast Beef	1	320	50	6	2	35	1300	47	24
Veggie Delite	1	230	25	3	1	0	510	44	9

Breakfast Sandwiches

Food Item	Amount	Total Calories	Fat Calories	Total Fat (g)	Sat. Fat (g)	Chol. (mg)	Sodium (mg)	Carbo (g)	Protein (g)
Bacon & Egg	1	320	140	15	4	185	520	34	15
Cheese & Egg	1	320	140	15	5	185	550	34	14
Ham & Egg	1	310	110	13	4	190	720	35	16
Steak & Egg	1	330	120	14	4	190	570	35	19
Western Egg	1	300	110	12	4	180	530	36	14

Food Item	Amount	Total Calories	Fat Calories	Total Fat (g)	Sat. Fat (g)	Chol. (mg)	Sodium (mg)	Carbo (g)	Protein (g)
6" Cold Sandwiches									
BMT	1	450	190	21	8	55	1790	47	23
Cold Cut Combo	1	410	160	17	7	55	1570	46	21
Seafood Sensation	1	380	120	13	4	25	1170	52	16
Tuna	1	430	170	19	5	45	1070	46	20
Deli Style Sandwiches									
Ham	1	210	35	4	2	10	770	35	11
Roast Beef	1	220	40	4	2	15	660	35	13
Savory Turkey Breast	1	210	35	4	2	15	730	36	13
Tuna	1	300	110	13	4	25	770	36	13
6" Hot Sandwiches									
Cheese Steak	1	360	90	10	4	35	1090	47	24
Chiptole SW Ch. Steak	1	440	170	18	6	45	1160	49	24
D. Tur. Br./Ham/Bac. M.	1	470	190	21	7	55	1620	48	26
Meatball	1	500	200	22	11	45	1180	52	23
Tur. Br./Ham/Bacon Melt	1	380	110	12	5	45	1610	47	25
Classic Club	1	390	190	21	10	0	1820	13	37
Atkins Friendly Wraps									
Chicken Bacon Ranch	1	440	230	26	9	90	1550	17	43
Mediterranean Chicken	1	350	160	18	5	60	1490	17	36
Turkey Bacon Melt	1	430	240	27	10	65	1870	20	34
Turkey Breast & Ham	1	390	210	23	8	60	1890	19	32
Atkins Friendly Salads									
Classic Club w/Kr. Ranch	1	590	380	43	14	220	2370	14	38
Gr. Ch. & Baby Spinach	1	620	440	48	13	215	1480	11	39
Salads									
Garden Fresh Salad									
w/BMT meats	1	290	170	19	7	55	1360	14	17
w/Cold Cuts	1	240	140	15	6	55	1140	14	15
w/Seafood Sens.	1	210	100	11	4	25	740	20	10
w/Tuna	1	260	150	17	4	45	640	14	14
Gr. Ch. & Baby Spinach	1	420	240	26	10	0	970	10	38
Mediterranean Chicken	1	170	40	4	2	55	520	11	22
6 grams of fat or less Salads (values do not include salad dressing or croutons)									
Garden Fresh	1	60	10	1	0	0	80	11	3
GF w/Chicken	1	160	30	4	0	45	580	14	17
GF w/Ham	1	120	25	3	0	25	840	14	12
GF w/Roast Beef	1	130	30	3	1	20	480	12	13

Food Item	Amount	Total Calories	Fat Calories	Total Fat (g)	Sat. Fat (g)	Chol. (mg)	Sodium (mg)	Carbo (g)	Protein (g)
GF w/Turkey Breast	1	110	20	2	0	20	580	13	12
GF w/Tur. Breast & Ham	1	130	25	3	0	25	800	14	14
GF w/Tur./Ham/R. Beef	1	160	35	4	1	35	870	14	18

Salad Dressings

Food Item	Amount	Total Calories	Fat Calories	Total Fat (g)	Sat. Fat (g)	Chol. (mg)	Sodium (mg)	Carbo (g)	Protein (g)
Atkins Sweet as Honey M.	2 oz.	200	200	22	3	0	510	1	1
Fat Free Italian	2 oz.	35	0	0	0	0	720	7	1
Greek Vinaigrette	2 oz.	200	190	21	3	0	590	3	1
Ranch	2 oz.	200	200	22	4	10	550	1	1
Red Wine Vinaigrette	2 oz.	80	10	1	0	0	910	17	1

Salad Fixings

Food Item	Amount	Total Calories	Fat Calories	Total Fat (g)	Sat. Fat (g)	Chol. (mg)	Sodium (mg)	Carbo (g)	Protein (g)
Bacon Bits	1	60	40	4	2	20	260	0	5
Croutons	1	70	30	3	0	0	200	8	1
Diced Egg	1	45	30	3	1	120	35	0	4
Garlic Almonds	1	80	70	7	0	0	65	3	3

Cookies

Food Item	Amount	Total Calories	Fat Calories	Total Fat (g)	Sat. Fat (g)	Chol. (mg)	Sodium (mg)	Carbo (g)	Protein (g)
Chocolate Chip	1	210	90	10	4	15	160	30	2
Chocolate Chunk	1	220	90	10	4	10	105	30	2
Double Chocolate	1	210	90	10	4	15	170	30	2
M & M	1	210	90	10	4	15	105	30	2
Oatmeal Raisin	1	200	70	8	2	15	170	30	3
Peanut Butter	1	220	110	12	4	10	200	26	4
Sugar	1	230	110	12	4	15	135	28	2
White Macadamia Nut	1	220	100	11	4	15	160	28	2

Fruizie Express (small)

Food Item	Amount	Total Calories	Fat Calories	Total Fat (g)	Sat. Fat (g)	Chol. (mg)	Sodium (mg)	Carbo (g)	Protein (g)
Berry Lishus	1	110	0	0	0	0	30	28	1
Berry Lishus (w/Banana)	1	140	0	0	0	0	30	35	1
Peach Pizazz	1	100	0	0	0	0	25	26	0
Pineapple Delight	1	130	0	0	0	0	25	33	1
Pine. Delight (w/Banana)	1	160	0	0	0	0	25	40	1
Sunrise Refresher	1	120	0	0	0	0	20	29	1

Soups (1 cup)

Food Item	Amount	Total Calories	Fat Calories	Total Fat (g)	Sat. Fat (g)	Chol. (mg)	Sodium (mg)	Carbo (g)	Protein (g)
Br. Wild Rice w/Chicken	1	190	100	11	4	20	990	17	6
Cheese/Ham/Bacon	1	240	140	15	6	20	1160	17	8
Chicken and Dumpling	1	130	40	4	2	30	1030	16	7
Chili Con Carne	1	240	90	10	5	15	860	23	15
Cream of Broccoli	1	130	50	6	0	10	860	15	5
Cream of Potato w/Bacon	1	200	100	11	4	15	840	21	4
Golden Broc. & Cheese	1	180	100	11	4	15	1120	16	5
Minestrone	1	90	35	4	1	20	1180	7	7

Food Item	Amount	Total Calories	Fat Calories	Total Fat (g)	Sat. Fat (g)	Chol. (mg)	Sodium (mg)	Carbo (g)	Protein (g)
New Eng. Clam Chowder	1	110	30	4	0	10	990	16	5
Roasted Chicken Noodle	1	60	15	2	0	10	940	7	6
Sp. Style Ch. with Rice	1	90	20	2	0	10	800	13	5
Tom. Gar. Veg. w/Rotini	1	100	5	0	0	0	900	20	3
Vegetable Beef	1	90	10	1	0	10	1050	15	5

Taco Bell®

Big Bell Value Menu

Food Item	Amount	Total Calories	Fat Calories	Total Fat (g)	Sat. Fat (g)	Chol. (mg)	Sodium (mg)	Carbo (g)	Protein (g)
Grande Soft Taco	1	450	190	21	8	45	1400	44	20
Double Decker Taco	1	340	120	14	5	25	800	39	15
1/2 lb. Bean Burrito Esp.	1	600	190	21	5	25	800	39	15
1/2 lb. Beef Combo Bur.	1	470	170	19	7	45	1610	52	22
1/2 lb. Beef/Potato Bur.	1	530	220	24	9	40	1670	65	15
Cheesy Fiesta Potatoes	1	280	160	18	6	20	800	27	4
Caramel Apple Empanada	1	290	130	15	4	5	290	37	3

Tacos

Food Item	Amount	Total Calories	Fat Calories	Total Fat (g)	Sat. Fat (g)	Chol. (mg)	Sodium (mg)	Carbo (g)	Protein (g)
Crunchy Taco	1	170	90	10	4	25	350	13	8
Taco Supreme	1	220	120	14	7	40	360	14	9
Soft Taco Beef	1	210	90	10	4.5	25	620	21	10
Ranchero Chicken Soft	1	270	130	15	4	35	790	21	13
Soft Taco Supreme Beef	1	260	130	14	7	40	630	22	11
Soft Taco Supreme Ch.	1	230	90	10	5	45	570	21	15
Grilled Steak Soft Taco	1	280	150	17	4.5	30	650	21	12
Double Decker Taco Sup.	1	380	160	18	8	40	820	40	15

Gorditas

Food Item	Amount	Total Calories	Fat Calories	Total Fat (g)	Sat. Fat (g)	Chol. (mg)	Sodium (mg)	Carbo (g)	Protein (g)
Supreme Beef	1	310	140	16	7	35	590	30	14
Supreme Chicken	1	290	110	12	5	45	530	28	17
Supreme Steak	1	290	120	13	6	35	520	28	16
Baja Beef	1	350	170	19	5	30	750	31	14
Baja Chicken	1	320	170	19	5	30	750	31	14
Baja Steak	1	320	150	16	4	30	680	29	15
Nacho Cheese Beef	1	300	120	13	4	20	740	32	13
Nacho Cheese Chicken	1	270	90	10	2.5	25	670	30	16
Nacho Cheese Steak	1	270	100	11	3	20	660	30	14

Chalupas

Food Item	Amount	Total Calories	Fat Calories	Total Fat (g)	Sat. Fat (g)	Chol. (mg)	Sodium (mg)	Carbo (g)	Protein (g)
Supreme Beef	1	390	220	24	10	40	600	31	14
Supreme Chicken	1	370	180	20	8	45	530	30	17
Supreme Steak	1	370	190	22	8	35	520	29	15
Baja Beef	1	430	250	27	8	30	750	32	14

Food Item	Amount	Total Calories	Fat Calories	Total Fat (g)	Sat. Fat (g)	Chol. (mg)	Sodium (mg)	Carbo (g)	Protein (g)
Baja Chicken	1	400	210	24	6	40	690	30	17
Baja Steak	1	400	220	25	7	30	680	30	15
Nacho Cheese Beef	1	380	200	22	7	20	740	33	12
Nacho Cheese Chicken	1	350	160	18	5	25	670	31	16
Nacho Cheese Steak	1	350	170	19	5	20	670	31	14

Burritos

Food Item	Amount	Total Calories	Fat Calories	Total Fat (g)	Sat. Fat (g)	Chol. (mg)	Sodium (mg)	Carbo (g)	Protein (g)
Bean	1	370	90	10	3.5	10	1200	55	14
7-Layer	1	530	190	21	8	25	1350	66	18
Chili Cheese	1	390	160	18	9	40	1080	40	16
Supreme Beef	1	440	160	18	8	40	1330	51	18
Supreme Chicken	1	410	130	14	6	45	1270	50	21
Supreme Steak	1	420	140	16	7	35	1260	50	19
Fiesta Beef	1	390	140	15	5	25	1150	50	14
Fiesta Chicken	1	370	100	12	3.5	30	1090	48	18
Fiesta Steak	1	370	110	13	4	25	1080	48	16
Grilled Stuft Beef	1	730	300	33	11	55	2080	79	28
Grilled Stuft Chicken	1	680	230	26	7	70	1950	76	35
Grilled Stuft Steak	1	680	250	28	8	55	1940	76	31

Specialties

Food Item	Amount	Total Calories	Fat Calories	Total Fat (g)	Sat. Fat (g)	Chol. (mg)	Sodium (mg)	Carbo (g)	Protein (g)
Tostada	1	250	90	10	4	15	710	29	11
Mexican Pizza	1	550	280	31	11	45	1030	46	21
Enchirito Beef	1	380	160	18	9	45	1430	35	19
Enchirito Chicken	1	350	130	14	7	55	1360	33	23
Enchirito Steak	1	360	140	16	8	45	1350	33	21
MexiMelt	1	290	140	16	8	45	880	23	15
Fiesta Taco Salad	1	870	430	48	16	65	1770	80	32
Fiesta Taco S. w/Shell	1	500	230	26	11	65	1520	42	25
Express Taco S. w/Chips	1	620	280	31	13	65	1390	60	27
Cheese Quesadilla	1	490	260	28	13	55	1150	39	19
Chicken Quesadilla	1	540	270	30	13	80	1380	40	28
Steak Quesadilla	1	540	280	31	14	70	1370	40	26
Zesty Ch. Border Bowl	1	730	380	42	9	45	1640	65	23
Zesty Ch. Bor. B. w/o Dress.	1	500	170	19	4.5	30	1400	60	22
Southwest Steak Bow	1	700	290	32	8	55	2050	73	30

Nachos and Sides

Food Item	Amount	Total Calories	Fat Calories	Total Fat (g)	Sat. Fat (g)	Chol. (mg)	Sodium (mg)	Carbo (g)	Protein (g)
Nachos	1	320	170	19	4.5	5	530	33	5
Nachos Supreme	1	460	230	26	9	35	800	42	13
Nachos BellGrande	1	780	380	43	13	35	1300	80	20
Pintos 'n Cheese	1	180	60	7	3.5	15	700	20	10
Mexican Rice	1	210	90	10	4	15	740	23	6
Cinnamon Twists	1	160	50	5	1	0	150	28	1

Food Item	Amount	Total Calories	Fat Calories	Total Fat (g)	Sat. Fat (g)	Chol. (mg)	Sodium (mg)	Carbo (g)	Protein (g)

Wendy's®

Sandwiches

Food Item	Amount	Total Calories	Fat Calories	Total Fat (g)	Sat. Fat (g)	Chol. (mg)	Sodium (mg)	Carbo (g)	Protein (g)
Classic Single w/Every.	1	410	170	19	7	70	920	37	25
Big Bacon Classic	1	580	270	30	12	100	1460	46	34
Jr. Hamburger	1	270	80	9	3	30	620	34	14
Jr. Cheeseburger	1	310	110	12	6	45	800	34	17
Jr. Bacon Cheeseburger	1	380	170	19	7	55	870	34	20
Jr. Cheeseburger Deluxe	1	350	140	16	6	50	860	36	18
Ultimate Chicken Grill	1	360	60	7	1.5	75	1100	44	31
Homestyle Ch. Fillet	1	540	190	22	4	55	1320	57	29
Spicy Chicken Fillet	1	510	170	19	3.5	55	1480	57	29

Side Selections

Food Item	Amount	Total Calories	Fat Calories	Total Fat (g)	Sat. Fat (g)	Chol. (mg)	Sodium (mg)	Carbo (g)	Protein (g)
Caesar Side Salad	1	70	40	4.5	2	10	190	2	6
Side Salad	1	35	0	0	0	0	20	7	2
Plain Baked Potato	1	270	0	0	0	0	25	61	7
Bacon & Cheese B. Potato	1	560	220	25	74	35	910	67	16
Broc. & Cheese B. Potato	1	440	130	15	3	10	540	70	10
Sour Cr. & Chive B. Pot.	1	340	60	6	4	15	40	62	8
Chili (small)	1	200	45	5	2	35	870	21	17
Chili (large)	1	300	70	7	3	50	1310	31	25
Shredded Cheddar Cheese	2 T.	70	50	6	3.5	15	110	1	4
Saltine Crackers	1 pkt.	25	5	0.5	0	0	80	4	1
French Fries (kids)	1	250	100	11	2	0	220	36	3
French Fries (medium)	1	390	150	17	3	0	340	56	4
French Fries (biggie)	1	440	170	19	3.5	0	380	63	5
French Fries (great biggie)	1	530	200	23	4.5	0	450	75	6

Homestyle Chicken Strips & Crispy Chicken Nuggets

Food Item	Amount	Total Calories	Fat Calories	Total Fat (g)	Sat. Fat (g)	Chol. (mg)	Sodium (mg)	Carbo (g)	Protein (g)
Homestyle Ch. Strips	3	410	160	18	3.5	60	1470	33	28
Deli Honey Must. Sauce	1	170	140	16	2.5	15	190	6	0
Spicy SW Chipotle Sauce	1	140	120	13	2	20	170	5	0
Heartland Ranch Sauce	1	200	190	21	3.5	20	280	1	0
Crispy Chicken Nuggets	4	180	100	11	2.5	25	390	10	8
Crispy Chicken Nuggets	5	220	130	14	3	35	490	13	10
Barbecue Sauce	1	40	0	0	0	0	160	10	1
Honey Mustard Sauce	1	130	100	12	2	10	220	6	0
Sweet and Sour Sauce	1	45	0	0	0	0	120	12	0

Garden Sensations Salads

Food Item	Amount	Total Calories	Fat Calories	Total Fat (g)	Sat. Fat (g)	Chol. (mg)	Sodium (mg)	Carbo (g)	Protein (g)
Mandarin Chicken	1	190	25	3	1	50	740	17	22
Crispy Noodles	1	60	20	2	0	0	170	10	1
Roasted Almonds	1	130	100	11	1	0	70	4	5

Food Item	Amount	Total Calories	Fat Calories	Total Fat (g)	Sat. Fat (g)	Chol. (mg)	Sodium (mg)	Carbo (g)	Protein (g)
Oriental Ses. Dr.	1	250	170	19	2.5	0	560	19	1
Spring Mix	1	180	100	11	6	30	230	12	11
Honey R. Pecans	1	130	120	13	12	0	65	5	2
House Vin. Dr.	1	190	160	18	2.5	0	730	8	0
Chicken BLT	1	360	170	19	9	95	1140	10	34
Home. Gar. Cr.	1	70	25	2.5	0	0	120	9	1
Honey Mus. Dr.	1	280	230	26	4	25	350	11	1
Taco Supreme	1	360	140	16	8	65	1090	29	27
Salsa	1	30	0	0	0	0	440	6	1
Sour Cream	1	60	45	5	305	20	20	2	1
Taco Chips	1	220	100	11	2	0	200	27	3
Homestyle Ch. Strips	1	450	200	22	9	70	1190	34	29
Creamy R. Dr.	1	230	200	23	4	15	580	5	1

Additional Salad Dressings

Food Item	Amount	Total Calories	Fat Calories	Total Fat (g)	Sat. Fat (g)	Chol. (mg)	Sodium (mg)	Carbo (g)	Protein (g)
Blue Cheese	1	360	350	38	7	30	350	1	2
French	1	250	190	21	3	0	670	13	0
French, Fat Free	1	70	0	0	0	0	300	18	0
Italian Caesar	1	230	220	24	4	25	350	1	1
Italian, Reduced Fat	1	80	60	7	1	0	690	6	0
Hidden Valley Ranch	1	200	180	20	3	25	410	3	1
H. Val. Ran. Dr., Red, Fat	1	120	100	11	2	20	470	4	1
Thousand Island	1	260	230	25	4	20	380	7	1

Frosty

Food Item	Amount	Total Calories	Fat Calories	Total Fat (g)	Sat. Fat (g)	Chol. (mg)	Sodium (mg)	Carbo (g)	Protein (g)
Junior	1	170	40	4	2.5	20	100	26	4
Small	1	330	80	8	5	35	200	56	8
Medium	1	440	100	11	7	50	260	73	11

"Combining commonsense advice with a vast amount of research that flies in the face of much conventional thinking, K.C. crushes widely held dangerous myths about health. He also shows you how to transform your health through optimal nutrition and practical lifestyle changes."

—JORDAN S. RUBIN, N.M.D., Ph.D., Author of *The Maker's Diet*

Super Health is a complete manual for physical, mental, emotional, and spiritual renewal. In these pages readers will find a simple, practical, step-by-step guide for unleashing the energy, health, and fitness that his or her body and spirit have been waiting for. Anyone can unlock the secrets of living healthier and longer... and enjoying it all the more. This "whole person" lifestyle program is based on solid scientific principles, and thousands of people have transformed their health through implementing these teachings into their lives. *The Seven Golden Keys* are: proper hydration, nutrition, exercise, managing stress, controlling and eliminating environmental toxins, achieving restorative sleep, and meditation and prayer.

"Timely and backed by solid leading-edge scientific evidence, *Super Health* truly speaks to the whole person. This information is life-transforming, easy-to-understand, and provides an empowering road map to a more vital life."

—DR. JOSEPH MERCOLA, Author of the *No Grain Diet*

SUPER-FOOD MEAL REPLACEMENT

LIVING FUEL Rx™ Super Greens and Super Berry™

Living Fuel Rx™ contains organic super foods and proven supplements, giving you full, balanced coverage of all your nutritional needs—all in one product. Nutrient-dense, low calorie, low glycemic, and high in antioxidants, Super Greens and Super Berry™ are used by people from every walk of life, from the health challenged to elite athletes.

Super Berry—each serving contains over 120 g of whole organic berries, including blueberries, strawberries, raspberries, and cranberries. It is a taste you're sure to love, and the nutrition you come to expect.

Super Greens—each serving is jam-packed with organic spirulina, spinach, kale, broccoli, carrots, and more.

HEALTHY FATS AND OILS

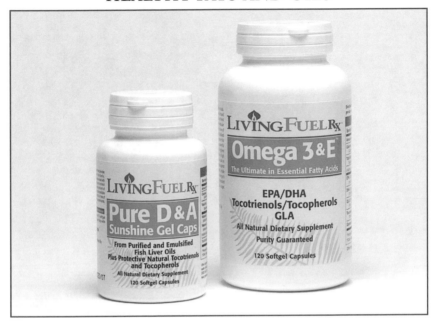

LIVING FUEL Rx™ Omega 3&E™

OMEGA 3&E™, antioxidant-protected fish oil caplets. OMEGA 3&E™ is a powerful combination of omega-3 essential fatty acids EPA and DHA combined with therapeutic doses of full-spectrum Vitamin E (including of tocotrienols and tocopherols) to provide antioxidant protection inside the body. Kept in its natural form throughout the production process and rigorously tested to ensure it is free from impurities, OMEGA 3&E™ is one of the safest and healthiest products of its kind.

LIVING FUEL Rx™ Pure D&A™ Sunshine Gel Caps

Pure D&A™ Sunshine Gel Caps is a safe and optimum source of Vitamin D for everyone in the family. An all-natural dietary supplement made from purified and emulsified fish oil livers, each softgel capsule contains the same amount of Vitamin D and Vitamin A found in one teaspoon of commercially available Cod Liver Oil. And Living Fuel Pure D&A™ is not factory made—it is all-natural, derived from mercury-safe fish.

HEALTHY SNACK LINE

LIVING FUEL Rx™ CocoChia Bar™

The CocoChia bar is a high energy, healthy fats product comprised of clean, organic fats, such as Coconut, Chia Seeds, Almonds and more. In a convenient and tasty bar form, the CocoChia bar is filling, delicious, and excellent for you. The ultimate multi-tasker…whether you're suffering from mid-afternoon munchies or require a quick refresher while traveling…the CocoChia snack bar is a smart choice.

LIVING FUEL Rx™ CocoChia™

CocoChia™ is a blend of two powerful super foods—organic Coconut and Chia Seeds. CocoChia is lightly sweetened with Therasweet®, Living Fuel's proprietary sweetener. Unlike other shredded coconut products, our coconut is **THE** product, not a byproduct of the coconut oil industry. We retain the coconut oil, which is where the true nutritional value lies, resulting in a higher quality and better tasting coconut product! Chia seeds are one of nature's perfect foods, containing essential fatty acids, protein, soluble fiber, protective antioxidants, minerals, and vitamins. CocoChia™ is the ultimate snack fuel—nutritious, low glycemic, anti-microbial and energy boosting.

SWEETENERS

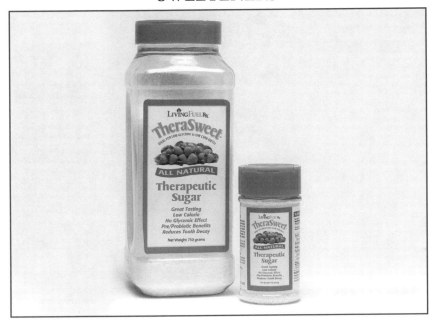

LIVING FUEL Rx™ TheraSweet™

TheraSweet™ is a safe and healthy alternative to the artificial sweeteners on the market today. Derived from organic and all-natural ingredients, it is an ideal sugar substitute for diabetics, those desiring weight loss, or anyone pursuing optimal health. With a sugar-like taste and texture, TheraSweet™ is a versatile sweetener that dissolves quickly and is heat stable for cooking and baking. TheraSweet™ is low calorie and has virtually no glycemic index.